The Trees of Eugene

Whitey Lueck

Cover photo: Bigleaf maple (*Acer macrophyllum*) dominates the riparian woodlands along the Willamette River that flows through the heart of Eugene. It was also the first tree to grace and shade the streets of early downtown Eugene in the mid-1800s. The maple's showy, pendulous flower clusters (shown here) appear in early April.

Photo taken by the author.

"Out of the trunk, the branches grow; out of them, the twigs.
So, in productive subjects, grow the chapters."

—from Chapter 63 of Herman Melville's *Moby-Dick; or The Whale*

CONTENTS

PREFACE

I never set out to write a book about the trees of Eugene. It just happened. During my early years in Eugene in the mid-1980s—at the start of what would turn out to be a lifetime of joy-filled *under-employment*—I spent a good bit of my abundant free time exploring the city's streets and alleys with my eyes on the trees. It was like a treasure hunt, as I sought the big, the beautiful, and the rare among our largest and longest-lived citizens. As my fascination with and knowledge about Eugene's trees grew, I decided to share it with others, and I also became a vocal advocate for the protection of our local trees.

In the mid-1980s, I taught my students about trees in the now long-defunct landscape program at Lane Community College. I became a member of Eugene's mayor-appointed Tree Commission around the same time. I put together three neighborhood "tree walk" brochures which the City of Eugene printed and made available to the public. And from 1989 through 1998, I led monthly TreeWalks for the general public from April through November, each month in a different part of Eugene.

Along the way, I also witnessed many changes—mostly for the better—in how our community cares for its trees. For example, I remember well into the 1990s that most tree care companies that advertised in the Yellow Pages (remember phone books?) listed "topping" as one of the services they provided. Topping—that is, the removal of all of a tree's major branches and trunks down to stubs—is not good for trees, and thanks to a long educational campaign, we seldom see it anymore.

Through the years, I also wrote several op-ed columns about trees for *The Register-Guard*, and many letters—to the newspaper, government agencies, private businesses, and individuals—extolling the benefits of trees and advocating for more thoughtful care of them. For ten years, from 1993 to 2003, I was the "gardening columnist" for *The Springfield News*—and its spinoffs called *Lane Living* and *Northeast Neighbor*—and some of my tree-related columns for those papers are included here. I was also the editor and lead contributor to *ETF News*—the quarterly newsletter of the Eugene Tree Foundation (now Friends of Trees)—from 1999 through 2013. The bulk of the essays in this volume were first printed in ETF's newsletters.

In 1997, I carried out a street-by-street inventory of trees on public property (between curb and sidewalk) in downtown Eugene, from 5th to 13th avenues, and from Lincoln to High streets. In 1998, soon after moving to Eugene's Amazon Neighborhood—where I still reside—I did a tree inventory from 24th to 30th avenues, and from Hilyard to Potter streets to determine the nature of the existing street-side tree population as well as to identify potential planting spaces for new trees. Then I put together a five-year plan for filling the many empty spaces with trees, which was completed by 2003 with the help of ETF volunteers, neighbors, and City of Eugene staff.

I also designed and led walking tours of the trees and forests of Eugene's three most heavily forested parks: Skinner Butte Park, Hendricks Park, and Spencer Butte Park. In 2005, the University of Oregon's Department of Landscape Architecture asked me to teach a course about trees that became my popular Trees Across Oregon course—affectionately known simply as TAO—which I've taught now for nearly fifteen years. And I've since added two more courses: The Nature of Eugene and Living Landscapes.

As time has passed—I'm now well into my fourth decade here in Eugene—I've learned some pretty amazing things about trees in general, and about Eugene's trees, in particular. The information gleaned through the years, however, has been scattered.

Because of my long association with so many aspects of Eugene's trees, I've sometimes been referred to around town as The Tree Guy—an appellation that makes me bristle just a little bit because I like to think that there's more to me than just trees. For example, here are a few of the other activities I've engaged in since my arrival in Eugene on the last day of June 1983:

- Taught Swedish for Linn-Benton Community College at its Corvallis campus
- Was a math tutor for elementary school students
- Served as a secretary in the chancellor's office of the Oregon State System of Higher Education
- Worked as a secretary for Moreland-Unruh Architects in Eugene
- Led tours of "new forestry" methods for the Willamette National Forest

- Operated for more than twenty years a small consulting business in landscape design, horticulture, and urban forestry
- Tutored French at Lane Community College
- Developed and taught (some of them multiple times) 80 *different* field classes in natural history throughout the West—from the Canadian Rockies to Mexico—first through Lane Community College (1986–2004) and then through my own OUT-OF-DOORS business (2005–2014)

So I hope I have herewith dispelled the myth that I am only The Tree Guy. But, anyway, back to trees. Having been affected my entire life by *dendrophilia*—or "the love of trees" in Greek—it is only fitting, as I approach The Finish Line of my life, that I collect some of my tree-related thoughts in one place, and that place is this little book. I hope you enjoy reading about Eugene's trees as much as I've enjoyed writing about them for so many years.

Whitey Lueck
Eugene, Oregon
January 2019

Nota bene: Because each article or chapter in this book was originally intended to stand alone, it's only natural that certain ideas or explanations are repeated. One example is my use of the word *cultivar*—which is usually followed here by an explanation of that word's origin, since it's a word that is unfamiliar to most people.

A LANDSCAPE TRANSFORMED: HOW TREES CAME TO DOMINATE THE LANDSCAPE OF THE EUGENE-SPRINGFIELD AREA

THERE ARE A NUMBER OF MYTHS about trees and forests that most Oregonians hold to be true. One of those myths is that, virtually everywhere west of the Cascade crest, since time immemorial, what we these days call "old-growth forests" have cloaked the hills and filled the valleys. And that landscape would still exist, had white settlers not arrived and cut the trees down to make way for farms and cities.

Contrary to this popular belief, the Euro-American settlers who arrived here in the upper Willamette Valley in the mid-1800s were greeted, not by cathedral-like conifer forests, but by mostly treeless prairies that extended across the entire valley floor and up into the nearby hills. Only near large watercourses such as the Willamette and McKenzie rivers did one find closed-canopy forests—of both broad-leafed trees (white alder, black cottonwood, and bigleaf maple) and conifers (mostly Douglas-fir and some grand fir).

Away from the river, however, and especially in the surrounding hills, trees occasionally grew both as solitary individuals and in groves of widely spaced trees with grass and wildflowers beneath them. Oaks (both Oregon white as well as California black) dominated this savanna landscape, but scattered conifers (Douglas-fir, incense-cedar, and ponderosa pine) were also present.

The three habitat types that formerly defined the upper Willamette Valley—grassland, savanna, and (in limited areas) forest—were the result of many millennia of landscape management by a series of fire-friendly cultures who had lived in the valley for over 10,000 years. These cultures' economies had come to depend on a productive and very open landscape that, unlike dense forests, provided an abundance of plants (roots, bulbs, fruits, seeds) and animals (deer, elk, waterfowl) that they gathered and hunted. For economic reasons, then, they annually set fire to the valley floor to maintain the open landscape that was so essential to their livelihood.

With the arrival of the agrarian and fire-*un*friendly Euro-American culture, a very different set of values was imposed on the local landscape. In the absence of frequent human-set fires, the surrounding hills quickly began to fill in with conifers—whose abundant, winged, wind-dispersed seeds and relatively fast growth rate enabled them to transform the hills in just a few decades from an open, oak-dominated landscape to a closed-canopy forest dominated by conifers.

Wolling (1884)

RESIDENCE OF JACOB GILLESPIE, 1 MILE NORTH OF EUGENE CITY, LANE COUNTY, OR.

This early-1880s view from Gillespie Butte toward the Coast Range—with horses grazing in the middle-ground on the future site of Valley River Center—clearly shows the still intact closed-canopy riparian woodlands of both broad-leafed trees and conifers along the Willamette River

Meanwhile, on the valley floor—where most of the pioneers chose to settle due to the superior quality of the soil for growing crops—people began to plant trees. The settlers, most of whom came from the Midwest, planted trees both for the food they could provide—fruits and nuts—as well as for their aesthetic and environmental benefits, including summer shade.

Trees such as the once-popular eastern black walnut "crossed the plains" as dried nuts in the wagons of the pioneers. These trees were valuable for their shade as well as for their delicious nuts, and one can still find individuals dating back to the 1800s gracing the front yards of old farmhouses. But fruit trees—most of which are grafted cultivars or cultivated (and named) varieties that cannot be propagated by seed—came to the Northwest as living plants and by boat from nurseries on the eastern seaboard.

Other useful trees such as the black locust—a fast-growing, very adaptable tree that provided fragrant flowers in spring, shade in summer, and rot-resistant fence posts after being cut down—were, like the nut trees, easily transported by seed, and popular around 19th-century farmhouses.

But early immigrants soon familiarized themselves with our area's native trees—as non-native "ornamental" trees were not yet available in local nurseries—and began to plant them. Conifers, especially Douglas-fir, were planted, but it was "shade" trees to cool the settlers' homes in summer, and still let the sun shine through in winter, that people really sought. Our native oaks, lovely as they are, were relatively slow-growing and somewhat difficult to transplant. And riparian species such as alder and cottonwood—though fast-growing and easy to transplant—simply never found favor with the settlers.

Only one indigenous tree species really fit the bill, and that was bigleaf maple—which settlers began to plant in great numbers on the valley floor, both around houses and along newly developed streets. The true-to-life drawings in A. G. Walling's *Illustrated History of Lane County*—published in 1884—clearly show young bigleaf maples along many Eugene streets.

The residence—at the corner of Broadway and Charnelton—of prominent early Eugenean, T. G. Hendricks, with its young, street-side bigleaf maples.

Over time, local nurseries began to provide an increasing variety of ornamental trees—non-native oaks, flowering cherries, lindens, magnolias, and many others—for local residents to plant both around their houses and along streets. Many of these plants, especially those from eastern Asia, had been "discovered" by plant explorers from Europe and America only in the late 1800s, and did not make their way into the nursery trade until well into the 1900s.

One of the artists for Walling's book sat on Skinner Butte and drew an overview of Eugene and its surroundings in the early 1880s (see below). That sketch clearly shows a sharp-tipped Spencer Butte in the distance—since then "rounded over" visually by the maturing Douglas-firs on its north flank—as well as young woodlands of both oak and conifer on Eugene's hills. Especially noteworthy in the sketch's foreground is downtown Eugene. Only thirty-some years after settlement, Willamette Street is lined with bigleaf maples, and conifers (likely all natives) and fruit and nut trees flourish around private residences away from the young community's main street.

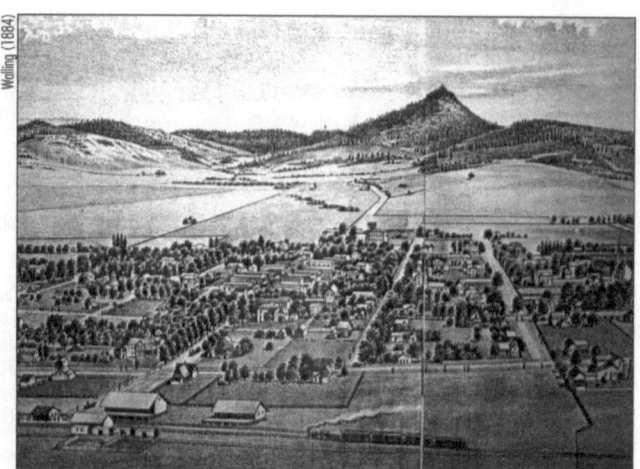

When looking out across the tree-filled city of Eugene these days, it is difficult to imagine that only 150 years ago the landscape was largely treeless.

Only a couple of decades after that sketch was made, however, the maples along Willamette Street were felled to make way for utility poles carrying electric and telegraph wires. Later still, after we began placing utility lines underground in the 1950s and 1960s, trees re-appeared along Willamette Street—but nothing (yet) to match the grandeur of the lovely allée of maples that graced the street for at least several decades in the late 1800s and early 1900s.

Over time, the planting of indigenous trees nearly ceased, as local nurseries procured and propagated more and more species of "exotic" trees that were more unusual or developed more spectacular autumn foliage or showier flowers than our local trees. Then, in the late 1900s, an interest in indigenous trees was renewed, at least to a limited extent. Young bigleaf maples—prohibited as street-side trees in most maritime Northwest communities because they "get too big"—began to be planted once again in Eugene when and where old street-side maples were removed.

On the slopes of the Chambers Overpass, a large planting of native conifers went in. And elsewhere in Eugene— along Amazon Creek and in East Alton Baker Park, for example—native trees were planted in great numbers to help restore native habitats that elsewhere in our communities have been displaced by both development (buildings, streets, parking lots) and the planting of non-native species.

This return to the planting of trees native to the upper Willamette Valley has been confined, so far, mostly to publicly owned lands—along streets and in parks and open spaces. In the coming years, however, perhaps it will spread to private property as well, as owners of residential and commercial properties learn about and begin to understand the ecological importance of planting indigenous trees and other plants.

From the mid-1800s until fairly recently, almost all of the trees planted in our communities were the result of caring individuals who simply wished to beautify their properties or neighborhoods, or benefit from the environmental advantages (largely shade) of trees. These days, public agencies and non-profits—including Friends of Trees—play a large role in the planting of trees, especially on public property. In recognition of the host of benefits provided by street-side trees, the City of Eugene has required since the late 1990s that all new neighborhoods include street-side park strips planted with trees that can over time develop large canopies— and that all commercial properties, including parking lots, include large-canopy trees. In many parts of Eugene, a quick comparison of older suburban streets and commercial areas with more recent developments shows clearly how far we've come in recognizing the importance of trees to our community's well-being.

These days, when looking down from any of the hills surrounding the communities of Eugene and Springfield, one can scarcely see the buildings for the trees. It is amazing to consider that the striking transformation from treeless grassland to urban forest occurred over a period of less than 150 years. Again, except for along the river, almost all of the trees growing on the valley floor were planted by humans. Conversely, virtually every tree we see on our now-forested hillsides developed there naturally.

But the view from atop the hills is not the only transformation that has occurred. Along with the dramatic change in the local landscape has come, over time, a change in our minds. Where once we planted trees almost exclusively for the benefits they provided to humans—fruits, nuts, shade, beauty—we are now seeing a slow but significant shift to viewing trees (and humans) as part of a much bigger picture that includes myriad plants and animals that are native to the upper Willamette Valley and with which we share this unique place. It remains to be seen how, in the long term, this shift will affect both us and the tree-dominated landscape that surrounds us.

(This article first appeared in the Winter 2012 newsletter of *Friends of Trees*.)

EUGENE-SPRINGFIELD'S OWN
FLAMING FOLIAGE FESTIVAL

I HAD THE PLEASURE OF SPENDING the single-digit years of my youth among the verdant, forest-covered mountains of northern Pennsylvania where, every fall, over a period of only a few weeks, the forests underwent an amazing transformation from the deep green of summer to a spectacular mix of yellow, orange, red, and purple.

(Did you know that Pennsylvania means "Penn's Woods," after the family of its Quaker founder, William Penn, and the Latin word for "forest"? The state was almost entirely covered by forest when Penn arrived in the late 1600s, and nearly seventy percent of the state is *still* forested!)

As lovely as the fall foliage was around Jersey Shore, the town where we lived, my family had a tradition of driving in mid-October to another small town about an hour away called Renovo, to attend that community's annual Flaming Foliage Festival. There, we sat outside on folding chairs on a sloping lawn, with the multi-colored mountains all around us, as the year's Flaming Foliage Queen and her court proceeded from behind the seated crowd to a small stage at the base of the slope. A brief ceremony took place during which the new queen was crowned by the previous fall's queen. Afterward, everyone applauded and we moved on to the other activities associated with the festival—including a drive into the surrounding mountains to ooh and ahh over the pretty colors.

I recall every year this early fascination with fall, when Eugene-Springfield's urban forest—in which I've lived now for most of my adult life—undergoes the same wonderful transformation. However, because we have a marine-influenced climate here in western Oregon, our falls, like our springs, are much longer than those in areas like Pennsylvania that have more continental climates. So instead of lasting only a few weeks, fall here extends from late September—when the katsuras, native to Japan, turn a pale yellow before dropping their leaves—to around Thanksgiving, when the foliage of Callery pears and Lavalle hawthorns becomes fiery red.

Perhaps the most stunning display in our area occurs most years during the first two weeks of October when local ash trees don their fall finery. Although our native Oregon ash (*Fraxinus latifolia*) can produce lovely, though relatively subdued hues ranging from pale yellow to almost orange, it is the cultivated, non-native ash species that garner the most attention in our urban forest.

Green ash (*F. pennsylvanica*) and white ash (*F. americana*) are the first two species to brighten our autumn days. Green ash is a medium-size tree native east of the Rockies that turns a brilliant yellow—in some years as early as the last week of September. In Eugene, showy plantings of green ash include the 600 block of Monroe Street and the section of Agate Street just north of Franklin Boulevard that leads to the Riverfront Research Park.

White ash—also native to the Midwest and the East—can eventually grow a bit larger than green ash, but has been planted in our area only since the early 1990s, so few trees have attained any real stature yet. (An exception is the remarkable three-trunked white ash on the University of Oregon campus, south of Deady Hall, which is by far the oldest white ash in our area.) In the wild, white ashes—depending on the individual—can range in fall color from bright yellow to almost purple. Most of the white ash cultivars (*culti*-vated *var*-ieties) we now plant, such as 'Autumn Purple' and 'Autumn Applause,' have simply stunning fall color that includes red or purple as well as orange and yellow all in the same tree!

The third cultivated ash, and the last to color up, is Mediterranean ash (*F. oxycarpa*), sometimes called Caucasian ash. It is the smallest of these three species, but can still attain 40 or more feet, especially when planted on the rich river loams found throughout much of the Eugene-Springfield area. This species also has the narrowest leaflets of the three ashes, creating a more finely textured canopy than either green or white ashes. The fall color of the most commonly planted cultivar of this ash called 'Raywood' ranges from burgundy on the outer part of the canopy to pale yellow in the interior.

All ashes are dioecious. That is, they bear unisexual flowers on separate trees. So an entire tree is either male (pollen-bearing) or female (seed-bearing). And since seeds are considered "messy" by so many people these days—and can also in some cases germinate and create a "weed problem"—every cultivar of the above three ash species is male. Or, if it is female, the seeds it produces are apparently sterile.

Ashes have pinnately compound leaves with a central axis off which leaflets occur in pairs, as well as a terminal leaflet. The leaves are arranged opposite one another along the twig. The number of leaflets per leaf generally ranges from five to seven, depending on the species.

Because wild ashes of these three species can vary considerably in their habit (the direction the branches grow) as well as form (the overall shape or silhouette of the tree), cultivars have been selected for superior habit and form as well as their fall color.

Fall would be amazing enough if our community were planted only with ashes. But we "celebrate diversity" around here, so there are still many more colorful deciduous trees to ogle, even after the ashes have dropped their last leaves.

(This article first appeared in the Fall 2012 newsletter of *Friends of Trees*.)

BOTANICAL NAMES HELP DIFFERENTIATE PLANT SPECIES AND VARIANTS

IF I WERE ASKED where one might acquire a "red maple," I would first need to ask a few questions before I could give the correct answer. Could it be the red maple that is native east of the Great Plains and has red flowers in late winter but green leaves all summer? Or maybe the red-leafed version of Norway maple, which is a horticultural variant of a maple species from Western Europe? Or the red-leafed form of Japanese maple, which is a common ornamental tree here in the upper Willamette Valley?

Once I could establish with certainty which maple my questioner meant, I would give her the botanical name of the tree so nurseries would know exactly which maple to procure for her. Thanks to an internationally recognized system of plant names, each cultivated plant species and its every variant has a single correct name. What a Swede calls a *lönn* is a *Spitzahorn* to a German, an *érable plane* to a French-speaking person, and a *Norway maple* to Americans. But a trained horticulturist in any of these countries knows the tree simply as *Acer platanoïdes*.

The botanical or scientific name of a plant consists of two parts: a capitalized genus name; and a species name written entirely in lowercase letters. And botanical names are always italicized or else written in plain text and underlined. The genus or "general" name is somewhat like our family names; the species or "specific" name is like our forenames. So if I were a plant, I would be called *Lueck whitey*. And just like our names, which are sometimes a bit unfamiliar—unless you're a Smith or a Jones—the genus names of most plants are often derived from ancient Latin or Greek names for the plant and may seem a bit odd at first.

But the species names are a little easier to understand, especially if you were fortunate enough to have had a little Latin or Greek in high school or college. Many species names are descriptive, even though they are written in Latin or Greek. For instance, *grandifolia* means "big-leafed" in Latin, as in *Magnolia grandifolia*, the southern magnolia frequently planted in our area. And *macrophyllum* means big-leafed in Greek, as in *Acer macrophyllum*, our wonderful, native bigleaf (!) maple.

Most of the trees and shrubs we grow in our yards also exist somewhere in the wild, so they have the same botanical names as their wild cousins. But most of our herbaceous plants (e.g., flowers and vegetables) are variants of their wild cousins that result from either many years of selection and hybridizing, or from a natural mutation that occurred in a nursery. These variants are properly called *cultivars*, which is short for cultivated variety, because they are varieties that do not occur in the wild. Cultivar names are usually in English and are always capitalized, written in plain text, and surrounded by *single* quotation marks. So that red-leafed Norway maple I mentioned earlier would be *Acer platanoïdes* 'Crimson King.'

Plant variants do occasionally occur in the wild, and these are indeed called *varieties*. A variety name follows the species name and, like it, is italicized (or written in plain text and underlined) and in lowercase letters. An example is the pink-flowering dogwood, *Cornus florida rubra*, which is sometimes seen growing wild in East Coast forests. Seeds planted from this variety "breed true" and develop into dogwoods with pink flowers just like the parent tree.

Cultivars, on the other hand, seldom breed true. That's why cultivars of ornamental plants are almost always vegetatively propagated (e.g., by dividing clumps of daylilies or taking cuttings of impatiens). And vegetable cultivars are usually produced by hybridizing two commercially uninteresting parents to produce the desired seeds. Only so-called *heirloom* vegetable seeds, in which there has recently been a resurgence in interest, will yield a nearly identical plant the next season from seeds collected from this season's plants.

If you've steered clear of botanical names in the past because they seemed too foreign and too long, remember that many of us feel fairly comfortable saying chrysanthemum and rhododendron, both of which are words of Greek origin that exceed ten letters in length. And to use most of the encyclopedic plant books that are available, such as Sunset's *Western Garden Book*, you need to look up the plant by its genus name, simply because the common names, as I illustrated above, can apply to two or more different plants.

Common names are still very useful, of course. For example, around here I seldom refer to bigleaf maples by their botanical name because most people know exactly which maple I mean. But when discussing plants with East Coast or European colleagues, I automatically refer to bigleaf maple by its botanical name, which is universally understood by horticulturists.

Unfortunately, the nursery and landscape industries have fallen prey over the past decade to the "dumbing down" that is so prevalent in other parts of our culture. Some of the people I meet these days who work with plants are unfamiliar with plant names, even in English. But that doesn't mean the rest of us need to give up. Knowing a plant by its name, spelling that name correctly, and writing it properly are, in my view, simply part of being civilized. Let's give three cheers, now, for *civilization*—which is itself a word of Latin origin that exceeds ten letters in length!

(This article first appeared in the 27 October 1999 edition of *The Springfield News*.)

KEEP COOL: GET A TREE

O N HOT SUMMER DAYS, I am happily reminded how effective large shade trees are at moderating summer temperatures, and at doing a lot of other things that make life more pleasant for those of us whose limbs end in fingers and toes, not in leaves.

Early pioneers to the southern Willamette Valley recognized the importance of planting trees that would grow big and provide shade and comfort. Many immigrants came from the Midwest or the East Coast, where trees lined streets and surrounded farmhouses as a matter of course. And when they arrived on the mostly treeless prairies of this area, they either nestled their homes among the few existing trees, or they made sure to plant trees, often bigleaf maples, as soon as the house was built.

Some of these planted trees still can be found. For example, at the east end of Willakenzie Road off Coburg Road, there is a spectacular pair of maples probably planted in the 1870s. The farmhouse is long gone, but the maples remain, becoming more magnificent with every year that passes.

One doesn't have to look far to see how effective trees are at attracting people on hot summer days. In parking lots that have trees, people will almost fight over the spaces that are shaded. Given the choice of walking down the sunny side of a street or the shady side, most people will choose the latter. And people who live on treeless streets or in homes with no trees around them throng to the area's shaded parks on hot days, where they are sure to find refreshment of the shady kind.

Trees help keep us cool in two ways. First, they intercept sunlight and prevent it from reaching surfaces that absorb it and radiate heat back to the surroundings. Second, during the growing season, trees are constantly pulling water in liquid form from the soil and transporting it to their leaves, where it passes out through small pores as water vapor, which is a gas.

When water changes from liquid form to vapor, it uses up energy or heat, and the air in the vicinity is actually cooled!

So trees act as giant air conditioners, cooling the air and of course cleaning it, too, as dirt and grime settle onto the leaves, to be washed to the ground the next time it rains. It goes almost without saying that a house surrounded by trees stays cooler in summer than a house with no trees around it. But not everyone wants to live in a deep, dark forest. And many of us like to have a sunny spot on the south side of the house for a vegetable garden.

Well, there is a way to keep cool at home and grow vegetables, too. Although the tendency is to plant shade trees for cooling directly south of the house, it is in fact more beneficial to plant them on the east and west sides of the house. The reason is that, for most of a summer day, the sun shines hardest against the east and west sides of the house. At midday, it does shine on the south side, but it's for a relatively short period and the sun at that time of day is quite high, so it doesn't have as great an effect on that side of the house as it does when it's at a lower angle, for a longer time, against the east and west sides.

So, by keeping the area south of your house treeless, you can get good light in the house, grow vegetables, and still get a considerable cooling effect from trees. Then on sunny winter days, when the sun is very low and closer to the southern horizon, it can really pour in the south side of your house, unhindered by any tree branches south of the house.

The past three summers, my home office became unbearably hot every afternoon because the large window by my desk faces west. Pulling the drapes didn't have much of an effect. But last winter, I transplanted a 15-foot-tall red alder to a spot about ten feet west of the window. It is amazing how much more comfortable my office is this summer because the alder, though still young, effectively prevents much of the afternoon sun from reaching the window and adjacent wall.

Next winter, when I'll really want to see every bit of sun there is, the leafless alder's branches will happily let most of the rays through to me. And I'll be smiling!

(This article first appeared in the 21 August 1993 edition of *Lane Living*.)

THE AMAZING GINKGO

THE MODERN GINKGO is an extraordinary tree that has changed little since its ancestors first graced the planet more than 200 million years ago—tens of millions of years before the advent of conifers (pines, spruces, etc.) and more than a hundred million years before broad-leafed trees (oaks, maples, etc.) became abundant. Although ginkgos have "broad" leaves, they are more closely related to conifers, as their seeds are not borne inside a "fruit" in the strictly botanical sense of the word.

Fossils of ancient ginkgos have been found in central Oregon; and in Washington, there's even a Ginkgo Petrified Forest State Park northeast of Yakima. But over many millions of years of changing climates, shifting continents, and the expanding ranges of other trees, ginkgos slowly disappeared until (apparently) they grew only in part of present-day China. Even there, they eventually became extinct in the wild—perhaps several thousand years ago—but have lived on as cultivated and often much-revered trees. The oldest living ginkgo in China is thought to be possibly 4,000 years old!

Ginkgos are dioecious, with male trees bearing only pollen and female trees producing the yellowish "fruit" inside of which is a white nut that encloses the actual seed. Although the seeds do not have much flavor, they have long been harvested and eaten in China, Japan, and Korea—and this writer has seen them for sale by the bushel-basket in San Francisco's Chinatown.

Although ginkgos grow in Eugene, they are uncommon and their growth here is slow compared to regions of the United States such as the mid-Atlantic states where the climate—with colder, drier winters and warmer, more humid summers—suits them better.

Toward the end of the 19th century, ginkgos were planted by the thousands in New York, Philadelphia, and other East Coast cities, because ginkgos, unlike most other trees, were tolerant of the then-severe air pollution afflicting those urban areas. Alas, as those trees reached "breeding age," thousands of female trees were cut down when they began dropping large quantities of slippery, smelly fruits onto those cities' sidewalks.

These days, all ginkgos sold by nurseries are grafted males—but mistakes happen, so there will probably always be a few girls around for all those lonely guys.

A close-up of the fan-like foliage and fully developed "fruits" of a "female" ginkgo.

(This article first appeared in the Fall 2009 edition of *ETF News*.)

COTTONWOODS ADD FRAGRANCE
TO SPRINGTIME

ONE OF THE MOST PLEASANT SCENTS in the tree world comes not from the tree's flowers, but from its aromatic leaves. Along local rivers, the fragrance of emerging cottonwood foliage is particularly striking. A whiff of it tells us that winter is truly over and spring is on its way.

Already in late February some years, the winter bud scales begin to fall from high in the cottonwoods. The scales have protected the cottonwood's flower buds as well as its vegetative or leaf buds from winter cold; both bud types were formed the previous year and then overwintered inside their sticky protective covers.

The sticky, fallen scales from cottonwood buds.

The first buds to open are the flower buds. Cottonwoods—like other members of the willow family (Salicaceae) such as aspen—bear their flowers in elongated clusters called catkins and are *dioecious* (dye-EE-shuss).

That is, male and female flowers are borne on separate trees. And because they are pollinated by wind rather than by insects, the "male" trees produce prodigious amounts of pollen. Depending on the weather, this pollen can be released over an extended period or during a fairly short time. If it is the latter, some human residents here in the upper Willamette Valley may experience an allergic reaction to the pollen. But as soon as rainy weather returns, as it usually does in March, the pollen count quickly goes down again.

As March advances, then, the cottonwoods conclude their flowering and begin to leaf out. That's when the real olfactory extravaganza begins. The leaves, like the bud scales themselves, are coated with a sticky substance that is very fragrant. In fact, in the journals of early pioneers in our area, cottonwoods are called "Balm of Gilead" trees, a biblical reference to a completely unrelated tree with similar "restorative" and fragrant properties that grows in the Middle East. To this day, some people— especially older and more rural area residents—refer to cottonwoods as "balm" or "bam" trees, both of which are simply diminutives of the original name. The rest of us call them cottonwoods—or *Populus trichocarpa.*

Young cottonwood leaves in early spring . . . you can almost smell them!

The fragrant foliage of cottonwoods persists into early summer, when the seeds of the "female" trees ripen and begin to float around in the wind, attached to their fluffy, cotton-like parachutes. If a seed should land on a suitable site (e.g., an open gravel bar along the Willamette River), it may germinate and start a new generation of trees. Unlike the large, heart-shaped leaves of older cottonwoods, young seedlings have long, oval-shaped leaves.

Then, throughout the summer here in the valley, the cottonwoods' canopies flutter wildly in the prevailing north winds, revealing the silvery-white undersides of the leaves and creating a soothing sound as well. Like "quaking" aspens, the petioles or leaf stalks of cottonwoods are flat in cross-section, so they move easily with the slightest breeze.

The biggest concentrations of cottonwoods occur along larger watercourses in our area such as the Willamette and McKenzie rivers because they need access to summer water to thrive. However, because of human activities associated with these rivers—the reduction of seasonal flooding, in particular, due to upriver dams—there are few appropriate sites anymore for new cottonwoods to get started. So the cottonwood population is aging, especially in urban areas where the rivers are the most severely controlled. Over time, the cottonwoods will likely disappear and those sites will be taken over by Oregon ash and bigleaf maple, both of which can germinate and grow beneath an existing forest canopy, unlike cottonwoods which need a "disturbed" and sunny site—such as a new gravel bar—for germination.

Fluttering cottonwood leaves exposing their silvery undersides are always a pleasing sight.

As wonderful a tree as the cottonwood is, it is not really appropriate in most residential and commercial landscapes—unless, of course, the site is near a river. Because of their exuberant growth, they tend to be weak-wooded, an attribute that is not "bad" in and of itself, but could cause serious problems near houses and other property. Moreover, because they need so much water, their roots will grow anywhere they can to get it and, in the process, those roots compete vigorously with other less aggressive plants you might be trying to grow nearby.

However, contrary to popular belief, cottonwoods are not a threat to sanitary sewer pipes unless those pipes already have cracks or breaks where a root might get in. But then, *any* kind of tree—not just cottonwoods—would do that just to tap into the yummy water and nutrients found inside the pipes!

Some older cottonwoods are prime nesting sites for great blue herons. These large wading birds nest colonially and require fairly substantial trees to support their heavy nests of twigs and branches. Although they will use other tree species for nesting, they seem to prefer cottonwoods. Ospreys, too, will nest in old cottonwoods with broken tops. And just north of Eugene, there is at least one bald eagle nest in the crotch of a large riverside cottonwood.

So when you are down by the river sometime this spring and remark on the "balminess" of the air—the word properly refers to the scent of the air, not its temperature—think kindly of these grand trees that grace our local riparian areas. Although you or someone you know may be allergic to the trees' pollen in spring, or you may find the cottony seeds to be a nuisance in early summer, remember that cottonwoods belong here in the upper Willamette Valley and they were here first.

Should they ever disappear, this part of the world would be a decidedly less fragrant place.

(This article first appeared in the Spring 2008 edition of *ETF News*.)

ALTERNATIVES TO A CHAINSAW MASSACRE

A FRIEND OF MINE WAS RECENTLY VISITED by a man representing a local tree service who recommended that she hire him to top the large maple growing alongside her house because, in his words, it was reaching a dangerous size. This friend, who herself knows a thing or two about trees and their proper care, looked back at the man and chirped, "Oh, but isn't that illegal?"

Indeed, in a growing number of communities across the United States, the topping of trees is forbidden on both public and private property. But not so here in Lane County. And frankly, I hope we never think we actually need a law to end this archaic practice. I would prefer to believe that once people acquire some understanding of the harm done by topping, the practice—like so many of the poor trees it's been done to over the past decades—will simply die out.

Many people once saw topping as the proper way to prune a tree. Some arborists even advertised it as one of the services they would provide! And customers who were interested in having the size of their tree's canopy reduced, for whatever reason, were delighted with the results. Their initial elation often soured, though, when after a few years the tree's canopy was just as big as before, and it had to be topped again. Eventually, people began to wonder if there weren't a less expensive way to care for trees.

A topped tree is not only unsightly, it also can create a safety hazard to nearby property and people. Along with it comes a never-ending maintenance nightmare, as the fast-growing shoots that develop following topping are more prone to wind breakage. And the large wounds topping creates provide entry points for rot organisms, so the tree declines rapidly in health and vigor.

So if topping is so awful (one billboard near Salem proclaims: "Topping is for pizza, not for trees!"), what's the alternative?

Option 1: If you find that your tree is truly in the way, one solution may be to "top" it . . . at ground level. If you'd still like a tree on that site, replace it with a species that doesn't grow as big, or plant it farther away from the house where it can mature gracefully and in good health.

Option 2: Have the tree pruned by thinning the canopy and perhaps reducing the crown. But understand that any crown reduction will only be temporary, as a young and healthy tree will soon compensate for the loss with new growth; mature trees, though, are more likely to stay more or less the same size if pruned properly. And remember that trees don't get "too big" any more than your well-nourished teenager gets "too tall." They just do what they're genetically programmed to do.

Many of us dendrophiles (that's Greek for tree-lovers) lean toward Option 3: If your tree was planted in a suitable location for its species in the first place, with adequate room for its canopy as well as its root system to develop, then perhaps it's best to leave it alone, or just remove the three D's (dead, diseased, and damaged branches) to ensure its continued health. Trees do sometimes fall over or drop limbs, but not just because they are "too big."

Be aware, too, that electric utilities are obligated by law to severely prune large-canopy trees that were planted under electric lines. It's an unfortunate situation for both the trees and the electric lines, and one that is going to take years to rectify. Meanwhile, kindly refrain from pestering too much the folks who do this. Try to focus instead on the fine work done by the City of Eugene's tree crews, for example, and many others.

If you're considering hiring an arborist, you might first call around to several companies and ask, "Hello, do you top trees?" If the answer is affirmative, consider responding like my friend in the first paragraph always does, with, "Oh, dear! Well, I guess I'll have to call someone else. Goodbye!" Over time, even the slowest learners should get the message.

(This article first appeared in the 5 February 1994 edition of *Lane Living*.)

LONG FALL BRINGS BRILLIANT COLORS
TO OREGON

OUTSIDE MY WINDOW, the first signs of fall color are evident in the Oregon ashes that have shaded the west façade of my house all summer. And the aspens, whose fluttering leaves have been a soothing presence these past months, are already starting to turn gold. In my view, summer is not ending; rather, fall is just beginning, and that is reason for celebration.

Unlike areas of North America with a more continental climate, where colorful fall foliage lasts only two or three weeks, fall color here in the maritime Pacific Northwest lasts more than two months. It begins in late September when the green ashes turn yellow and doesn't really end until the cottonwoods along the rivers have lost all of their leaves around Thanksgiving or even later. What a treat!

I'm already preparing myself for the annual barrage of dismissive comments from immigrants who came here from New England and the upper Midwest, who claim that "their" fall is more spectacular than "ours." How spectacular is spectacular enough? And why do we think we have to compare natural phenomena anyway? It just seems so silly.

Having grown up in Pennsylvania and attended graduate school in Wisconsin, I am very familiar with and appreciative of the autumnal display provided by the magnificent hardwood forests east of the Great Plains. It is, in a word, glorious. But a forest of Douglas-firs and western hemlocks is a lovely sight, too, in fall. Vine maples in the forest undercanopy turn yellow; Pacific dogwoods growing at the forest's edge turn pink; and the moss-covered trunks of bigleaf maples hold aloft their crowns of gold. These brightly colored deciduous plants create an especially handsome picture against the backdrop of evergreen conifers whose cinnamon-brown trunks and deep green foliage provide the perfect contrast.

From the Coast Range to the Cascades, vine maple lends sparkle to much of western Oregon's landscape at this season. Interestingly, although it turns yellow on shaded sites, it turns bright red when it grows on sunny hillsides, at the edge of forests, or in the lava flows of the High Cascades. That's because its leaves produce large amounts of anthocyanin pigments— the same pigment that gives beets their characteristic red color—when exposed to the sun. Vine maples that grow in the shade produce mostly xanthophyll pigments which are yellow. Both the red and yellow pigments are masked throughout the growing season, however, by the more abundant and green-colored chlorophyll pigment. With the arrival of cooler weather and longer nights in fall, the chlorophyll breaks down and the other pigments that were hidden all summer finally become visible. And what a show it can be.

Vine maple (*Acer circinatum*) is a shrub, not a tree, because it almost always grows in multi-stemmed clusters and no individual trunk ever gets very big. Moreover, the slender trunks of older vine maples, unable to support a great deal of weight, eventually bend over to the ground, sometimes rooting again and giving rise to another maple cluster. It is this peculiarity that apparently gave rise to the common name of vine (or sometimes "viney") maple.

This shrub is one of very few plants native to western Oregon that is readily available in local garden centers and nurseries. Sometimes the plants are grown from seed, but often they are collected in the wild and then placed in containers for sale. Older plants that were dug in the wild often undergo a lengthy period of adjustment in the garden after being replanted. I prefer to purchase younger, more vigorous plants—preferably those grown from seed rather than collected—that will experience very little "transplant shock" and are ready to grow.

Although vine maples will survive being planted in full sun on the floor of the southern Willamette Valley, they do better in shadier locations or at least near a large shrub or tree or building that will provide some protection from the hottest summer sun. Maples planted in the open will develop a very upright habit (i.e., most of their trunks will be nearly vertical) and smaller leaves; those planted on shadier sites will develop a more spreading habit and larger leaves.

On most sites, newly transplanted vine maples need supplemental water during the establishment period. That means you'll need to water them several times a month during our summer drought, for two seasons, until they recover from the shock of transplanting. After that, the maples should do just fine on their own. If they do fail to thrive, though, you can usually blame the site rather than your horticultural ability. And some vine maples get a twig blight that kills back part of the plant, but such plants often re-sprout from the base.

The Big Show that vine maples put on every fall begins in mid- to late-September on the lava flows of the Cascades. One of my favorite spots at that time is near the junction of Highways 126 and 20, not far from Fish Lake. And during the first week of October, the vine maples along Highway 242's so-called Dead Horse Grade—where all the hairpin curves are—are simply stunning.

By late October, maples at lower elevations have reached their peak. And most years, in early or even mid-November, one can still find lovely vine maples along valley bottoms in the western Coast Range (e.g., along the Siuslaw River near Whittaker Creek Campground). So if you happen to miss The Early Show in the High Cascades, check out The Late Show closer to the coast. You won't be disappointed.

(This article first appeared in the 27 October 2001 edition of
The Springfield News.)

IN PRAISE OF BIGLEAF MAPLES

B EFORE THE ARRIVAL OF EURO-AMERICAN SETTLERS in this area, bigleaf maple was a major component of local woodlands that ranged in extent from a narrow riverside fringe to a substantial forest stretching up to a half-mile or more away from the river. Trees growing near the river were less likely to burn during the annual fires set by local aborigines that kept the rest of the valley floor landscape mostly open and treeless. And maples in particular are known to slow and even stop a wildfire because their big, relatively lush leaves are less flammable than the resin-filled needles of conifers.

Early settlers planted bigleaf maples around their farmhouses and along their lanes to provide welcome shade during the summer. And as Eugene City grew, bigleaf maples became the preferred street trees because they were easy to transplant and grew very fast on the deep river loam that underlies much of the downtown area.

When electricity arrived in Eugene, many of the by then decades-old maples that shaded downtown streets were removed to make way for utility poles and wires. As the 20th century progressed, many other maples were felled for a variety of reasons and very few were replanted. Instead, trees from other parts of the world (e.g., Norway maple, northern red oak, and Japanese flowering cherry) began to be planted, as they were readily available from local nurseries and, according to some detractors, bigleaf maple "just got too big."

It wasn't until the 1980s that sentiments toward bigleaf maples began to change, when city arborists and planners recognized that this species was indeed one of the best for Eugene neighborhoods with deep, fertile river loam. In fact, bigleaf maple is one of the most drought-tolerant maple species in the world, a real plus in the face of our annual summer drought, and now climate change.

Because bigleaf maple is grown nowhere else outside the maritime Pacific Northwest, and because no other regional city has chosen to plant the species in any great numbers, Eugene stands alone as a proponent of this mighty native tree. As older maples continue to be removed because of disease or concerns about public safety, current City policy ensures that these sites will be replanted with bigleaf maples, so Eugeneans of the twenty-second century will have the same opportunity we have to behold a glorious canopy of maple leaves arching over streets and parks throughout much of the community.

And what else are bigleaf maples good for? Here, a bigleaf maple necktie—with attached collar of sensuously soft thimbleberry foliage—affords just the right amount of protection from prying eyes, while still providing plenty of exposed skin for that nice, all-body tan. (Taken in summer 1978, this photo was not part of the original newsletter article.)

(This article first appeared in the Winter 2000 edition of *ETF News*.)

SOME TREES DON'T GET
A WINTER VACATION

HERE IT IS MID-WINTER—the first week in February, which is midway between the winter solstice and the spring equinox—and many of Eugene's trees are hard at work, making the world a better place. (And you thought trees were "dormant" during the winter!)

Needle-leafed evergreen trees or "conifers" work the hardest during the winter. For example, Douglas-fir (*Pseudotsuga menziesii*) and Norway spruce (*Picea abies*) are photosynthesizing every chance they get, taking water and carbon dioxide and making sugars and oxygen whenever the temperature is above freezing. No, they are not putting out new needles or adding wood to their trunks, but they're working nonetheless.

And although spring is still nearly two months away, some conifers have already completed their reproductive activities, so to speak, for the year. The pollen cones of both coast redwood (*Sequoia sempervirens*)—which is not native to the Willamette Valley—and the native incense-cedar (*Calocedrus decurrens*) ripened during the month of January and shed their pollen which floated through the air to fertilize the future seed cones elsewhere in the tree's canopy or on another tree.

The redwood's pollen cones persist on the tree for many weeks, but those of incense-cedar are dropped soon after completing their job. They are dull yellow in color and under some incense-cedars create a golden carpet for a few days after falling.

Some broad-leafed deciduous trees begin flowering during the second half of winter and well before their leaves emerge. Examples include red maple and silver maple, and American elm and Siberian elm. By far the showiest-flowered of these four tree species is the red maple, which is also the most commonly planted of the four.

28

Many people think that red maple (*Acer rubrum*) is so named for its fall color, but in fact it's the color of its late winter flowers that gives the tree both its species name (*rubrum*, from the Greek for red) as well as its common name. Most of the red maples we plant in our area are cultivars—that is, *culti*-vated *var*-ieties, or mutations that occurred naturally and that are propagated by grafting—with foliage that turns red in fall, such as 'October Glory' red maple. But where the trees grow wild, east of the Great Plains, fall foliage color ranges from yellow through orange to red.

In the wild, flower color is usually a muted red or pink. But most of the red maple cultivars we plant in our area have deep red or even scarlet flowers that are difficult to miss when in bloom—unless you happen to be colorblind, which many men are.

Red maple in flower.

Although red maples are common throughout our community—and elsewhere in the maritime Northwest—there are exceptionally large concentrations of them in downtown Eugene around the Hult Center and along both sides of Olive Street between 8th and 10th avenues. (It is interesting to note that the trees along Olive were planted in 1993 inside cylindrical metal "root barriers," the ostensible purpose of which was to force the trees' roots to grow deeper into the soil, to prevent the roots from lifting sidewalks and curbs. The roots of some of the trees have been able to escape through the bottom of the barriers—so the trees have developed normally—but most of the maples have not been so fortunate. Compare for yourself the relative vigor of the red maples in these two blocks and be thankful that these cursed corsets of corrugated metal were not, as far as I know, used elsewhere in Eugene.)

So keep your eyes open for the signs of spring in the tree world, even though it is still winter until March 20th. And remember: Although some trees do truly "sleep" through the dormant season, others are diligently engaged in very important work, whether or not it's noticeable to casual passersby.

Incense-cedar pollen cones open in January.

(This article first appeared in the Winter 2009 edition of *ETF News*.)

THE STORY OF DOUGLAS-FIR

NOWHERE ELSE IN THE WORLD does a single tree species so dominate a forested region as Douglas-fir does here in the maritime Pacific Northwest. But this role is a relatively new one for Douglas-fir. Although it appears in the fossil record as far back as 15 million years ago, it appears to have been uncommon in regional forests until about 12,000 years ago, toward the end of the most recent Ice Age.

Douglas-fir (*Pseudotsuga menziesii*) is named for David Douglas, the Scottish horticulturist sent to the Northwest in the early 1800s to collect "interesting plants" to introduce to British gardens. It is not a "true" fir like noble fir and grand fir (both of the genus *Abies*), hence the hyphen in its common name. Nineteenth-century botanists were in fact uncertain whether the tree was a kind of hemlock (genus *Tsuga*) or spruce (*Picea*). Eventually, however, they decided to place the tree in an entirely new genus they called *Pseudotsuga*, or "false hemlock." Its species name honors Archibald Menzies, a Scottish naval surgeon and botanist (a common dual-vocation in those days) who accompanied George Vancouver on his Pacific Northwest exploration in the early 1790s, and who was the first European to describe the tree.

Conifers, or cone-bearing trees, first developed during the Jurassic period 190–140 million years ago but didn't reach their peak dominance on the planet until the Cretaceous period 140–65 million years ago. Since that time, conifers have been in continuous decline worldwide, with most species that once existed already having become extinct. Our rich, conifer-dominated forests here in the Northwest are truly the last stronghold for conifers. And, interestingly, Douglas-fir, a very recent arrival upon the conifer scene, is by far the most common of the many different conifer species here in the Northwest.

Yet forest ecologists refer to this land dominated by Douglas-fir—from the Pacific to an elevation of about 3,500 feet in the West Cascades—as the Western Hemlock Zone. Why is that? Forested zones are generally named for the tree species that, in the absence of disturbance (e.g., fire, disease, clear-cutting) would eventually dominate the upper canopy of a region's so-called climax forest. In our area, that species is western hemlock (*Tsuga heterophylla*).

But doesn't Douglas-fir dominate the canopy in undisturbed forests? Yes, but the undercanopy of those forests is mostly western hemlock, with not a Douglas-fir to be seen (Douglas-fir seeds are unable to germinate on moss- and needle-covered soil). So as the old Douglas-firs that now dominate the canopy slowly die out, they are replaced by western hemlocks.

So why aren't there any forests in western Oregon and Washington where we *see* this? Ahh! That's because the stage of forest succession that is dominated by large, old Douglas-firs (what we these days call old-growth forests) can last for several centuries, since Douglas-fir is very long-lived. And during that long period of time, there is bound to be a forest fire that will start the whole cycle over again, well before western hemlock gets to assume dominance in the upper canopy.

A very common misconception is that an old-growth forest is a *climax forest*; that is, in the absence of disturbance, an old-growth forest will remain like that in perpetuity (like tropical rainforests, which are indeed climax forests). But old-growth is just a stage—albeit a very long one—that area forests go through on their way to becoming climax forests. However, because of our region's winter-wet and summer-dry climate and the near certainty of a catastrophic fire over a period of several hundred years, the climax stage is just never reached.

Old-growth forests began to develop during only the past 5,000 years or so. Before that time, although Douglas-fir was already very abundant, the forests were more open and likely burned more frequently due to the warmer and drier climate (relative to today's) that prevailed during that period.

So perhaps we need to reconsider the use of the relatively recently coined term "ancient" forests. Again, Douglas-fir has dominated our region's forests for about the same brief amount of time that humans have lived in this part of the world (ca. 12,000 years). And the old-growth ecosystem has been around for less than half that long.

Here in the Eugene area, closed-canopy Douglas-fir forests are an even more recent phenomenon. Because local aborigines set fire to the landscape on a regular basis, closed-canopy forests were able to develop only in the vicinity of larger watercourses like the Willamette and McKenzie rivers. And these forests seldom lasted for a very long period, due to occasional and sometimes catastrophic floods. Away from the rivers, the landscape was largely treeless prairie, or savanna with widely scattered trees (mostly oak, with some ponderosa pine and Douglas-fir).

The forests that now cloak parts of Eugene's south and east hills have developed only in the past 150 years. Seeds borne by the scattered conifers that already grew in the area in the mid-1800s quickly took hold on the open slopes of these hills, following the termination of human-set fires.

As impressive as some of Eugene's forests are these days, none of them is an old-growth forest. Stands on the north slopes of Skinner Butte and Spencer Butte certainly have some large trees in them, but they lack other features characteristic of old-growth forests, most notably an undercanopy of small- and medium-sized conifers of a species other than Douglas-fir (e.g., western hemlock, or possibly grand fir).

Many of us think that, before the arrival of European-Americans, the landscape of western Oregon had existed unchanged for many thousands, if not millions, of years. But even before the elimination of frequent, human-set fires and the introduction of non-native tree species, regional forests were in a constant state of flux due to periodic climatic changes and the influence of the series of human cultures that preceded our own.

The signature seed cones of Douglas-fir, with three-pronged "bracts" protruding from among the cone scales.

(This article first appeared in the Spring 2004 edition of *ETF News*.)

THE FUTURE OF DOUGLAS-FIR IN EUGENE

AS DISCUSSED IN THE SPRING 2004 edition of *ETF News*— The Story of Douglas-fir—our state tree is a relatively new arrival here in western Oregon, having become abundant only in the last 12,000 years. The old-growth forest ecosystem developed during only the past 5,000 years or so. And here in Eugene, the hills became cloaked with Douglas-fir very recently, after the termination of aborigine-set fires about 1850, when the trees began to seed in from widely scattered Douglas-firs that already grew in the area.

Currently, most of the firs in Eugene are 100–150 years of age, especially in forested areas such as Spencer Butte Park, and the north side of Skinner Butte. Here and there, one can find older trees, such as the possibly 400-year-old behemoths near Spyglass, some scattered trees along the ridgeline, a couple of old firs at Riverridge Golf Course, etc. And a small number of younger firs have been planted on private property and along streets.

These days, however, hardly anyone plants Douglas-fir within the City limits and City ordinance generally forbids the planting of any conifers along streets. When firs in the hills are cut to make way for new houses and streets, they are seldom replanted; instead, people plant small "ornamental" trees such as flowering cherries, Japanese maples, and birches. And when new parks are developed on the valley floor, we sometimes plant a few firs in them, but nothing that will ever develop into a real forest.

Interestingly, when the first Euro-American settlers arrived in the mid-1800s, most of the firs in the future Eugene City grew along the river. Drawings made in the early 1880s clearly show hundreds of lofty firs still poking their heads above the riparian woodlands, but these, too, were eventually cut. Few firs grew in the hills. Now, it's just the opposite.

Of course, landscapes are constantly changing, and what one sees at one moment is merely a snapshot in time; it will never look exactly like that again. But with so few new firs being planted and the older ones getting yet older with every year that passes, we need to think about how the landscape is changing, and if these changes are desirable.

Douglas-fir belongs here in the upper Willamette Valley and future Eugeneans deserve to walk through woodlands of 150-year-old firs just as we do right now. But if the citizens of 2150 are to do that, we need to be planting those forests now. And if they are to walk through mixed-age fir woodlands of, say, 150- and 300-year-old trees, we need to be creating gaps in the existing woodlands and planting those gaps with young firs.

You might think, "Douglas-fir monocultures in *my* city? No way!" But nearly 100 percent of the trees in the Hendricks Park forest are firs, and they planted themselves. That's just what happens in western Oregon. Here and there in the ridgeline forest, we find a few incense-cedars and valley ponderosa pines (and an occasional grand fir), but Douglas-fir naturally dominates these forests and we need to bear that in mind when planning for the future.

So how can we ensure that Eugene 150 years from now will still have plenty of Douglas-firs, both scattered individuals and groups as well as young woodlands? Let's start by planting firs on the valley floor. In the past decade, a few have been planted along new sections of the riverside bike path and elsewhere such as Rasor Park, but these areas could use many, many more. There are plenty of open, sunny spots—which firs need to grow vigorously—on both sides of the river.

What about Sladden Park, which is currently dominated by a lovely stand of century-old firs? The open area in the west end of the park could be planted to new firs and, as the older firs decline or fall, they too can be replaced with the same species. In new parks on the valley floor, sections could be designated for *afforestation* (the planting of future forest where there was none before) instead of devoting the entire park to more conventional ornamental plantings or just a few scattered firs. Again, if Eugene in the future is to have vigorous, young fir forests, we need to plan for them and plant them, because they just aren't going to happen naturally anymore.

There are also huge, publicly owned areas along local highways that could be afforested, from the I-5/I-105 interchange to the Northwest Expressway. The southern part of I-205 around Portland is beautifully "firred" (and "mapled") because the trees were already there before the road was built and they were retained. Just because there are no trees along Eugene's highways now doesn't mean we have to be content with this ugliness forever. Just hire a reforestation (or *afforestation!*) crew and get the trees planted.

In the South Hills, residents and developers need to be encouraged (required?) to replant firs when old ones are removed. We Eugeneans love the conifer-clad hills that embrace the east and south edges of our community, but the appearance of those hills is changing as development continues to bite holes in the existing fir canopy.

What about the forested ridgeline parks themselves? Perhaps we need to "manage" these forests a bit more rather than just letting them be. Right now, our community is in preservation mode, but that may not be the best thing in the long run for these forests. Many forested municipal parks in northern Europe (e.g., Germany and Sweden) are "working" forests where the cutting of trees is an acceptable and desirable part of forest care.

Here in Eugene, we might open some gaps in the existing woodlands and get a second tier or generation of trees started. Very dense stands might be thinned to improve the health of the remaining trees. We know how to do this kind of "gentle" forestry and doing it right in our own backyard would be a great way to demonstrate a responsible, long-term approach to caring for City forests and provide a nearby educational opportunity that Eugeneans might not otherwise get.

Douglas-fir deserves to be an important part of Eugene's landscape for many decades, and perhaps centuries, yet to come. As existing woodlands age, the ridgeline is chopped up into smaller and smaller groups of firs, and if few new firs (and no new fir woodlands) are planted, Eugene's landscape will change dramatically. We can let that happen, or we can develop a plan for a more fir-filled future that will return firs to the riverside corridor, plant new woodlands, and create healthier and more ecologically diverse forests along the ridgeline.

(This article first appeared in the Summer 2004 edition of *ETF News*.)

GETTING RID OF UNWANTED STUMPS

AT ONE TIME OR ANOTHER, most of us have to deal with a tree or shrub that has died or, for whatever other reason, must be removed from our yard. The removal of the above-ground part of the plant is pretty straight-forward. You just saw it up into pieces until there's nothing left but the stump. But then what?

As usual, different people will go about removing a stump in different ways. For the pickup crowd—with or without a winch—there's the rip-and-haul method. This technique works well enough with many shrubs, but it is seldom applied to trees. And when it occasionally is, what's ripped is not the *tree* out of the ground, but the *bumper* off of the truck—uh-oh!

Then there are those of us who will hire someone with a "stump grinder" machine to come in and for a certain sum per inch diameter of the stump, grind out its topmost part, then backfill the hole with soil. That's easy enough and it looks nice afterward, but it can cost a pretty penny, depending on the size of the stump. And access to the big machine may be difficult in a small yard, plus there's all that noise and grime.

Some prefer to use p-o-i-s-o-n, which is typically marketed with a charming name like "stump killer." All you have to do is pour the herbicide onto the stump's freshly cut surface and watch it die. Although usually effective, this approach involves the purchase of a highly toxic substance, the use of it in an exposed area of the garden, and then the storage or disposal of whatever's left in the bottle. No thanks.

One option that is seldom considered is leaving the stump right where it is! There are two reasons why we usually don't consider this option. First, unless the plant was already completely dead, we're afraid that it will resprout from the stump. And second, we may find the stump unsightly, so we want it removed for aesthetic reasons.

With regard to the first concern, most conifers (e.g., Douglas-fir, pines, and juniper) cannot sprout from the stump. The exceptions are coast redwood, China-fir (*Cunninghamia*), and yew (*Taxus*)—none of which is common in our area. And the only reason that the stumps of broad-leafed plants (rhododendrons, maples, etc.) will sprout is that special "dormant" buds right beneath the bark of the stump are stimulated by sunlight to begin growing once the rest of the plant has been removed.

So don't let the dormant buds see the sun! Cut the stump off as close to the ground as possible, then cover it with a piece of cardboard, sprinkle some leaves or other mulch on top to hide the cardboard, and voilà! The plant will think the sun has burned out, and that'll be the end of that. By the time the cardboard rots, the stump will be dead.

The concern about aesthetics is, as usual, a bit more difficult to address. But if the stump is in an existing shrub bed, still-living plants should quickly grow in to fill the space and hide the stump. Or, if you really need to plant a new plant in that space, just place it *next* to the stump instead of right where the now-absent plant grew.

If the stump is in the middle of a turf area, you can still use the cardboard trick and then plant something such as nasturtiums to at least temporarily hide the spot. Or plant another shrub or tree nearby. If you choose to replant a new tree or shrub right next to the old one's stump, the new plant's roots will quickly occupy the soil channels where the old roots are rotting away, often making it easier for the new plant to get established.

And by leaving a stump in the ground, rather than removing it, we avoid disturbing the soil, which is good not just for the soil, but for our arm and back muscles that would have to regrade the area.

So next time you face the question of what to do with a stump, remember that, in addition to the rip, grind, and poison methods, there is Another Way. It's not always going to be the way to go, but it is often an acceptable and practical alternative.

(This article first appeared in the 24 July 1996 edition of
The Springfield News.)

BETWEEN CURB AND SIDEWALK:
WHERE STREET TREES GROW

THEY HAVE DISAPPEARED from most of downtown Eugene. Older neighborhoods generally have the nicest ones. Subdivisions constructed between the 1960s and 1990s typically have none. What are they? They are the publicly owned strips between the curb and sidewalk, where most of our street trees grow.

Legend has it that these strips came into being in the eastern United States back in the 1880s to serve as temporary storage areas for snow that was removed from streets after winter storms. Pedestrians could thus continue to use the set-back sidewalks instead of being forced to walk in the cleared streets, and they could also be better protected from slush and water (depending on the season) splashed up by passing vehicles.

Over time, people began to plant trees in these strips to shade and beautify their neighborhoods. These days, in many communities, some of the most valuable residential real estate is along those streets with wide strips and mature trees. Eugene's University Street between 19th and 23rd avenues is a good example.

And what is this area between curb and sidewalk called? Around here, most people refer to it as the *parking strip*. Elsewhere in the United States, it has a great variety of names including *the parking, park strip, parkway, greenway, boulevard, boulevard strip, planter bed, planter strip*, and *tree lawn* !

Because we don't usually park cars on it—and to do so compacts the soil and harms the trees—it seems wrong to call it a *parking strip*. My personal preference is to call it a *park strip*. The generally long and narrow area is indeed strip-like. And because it is a publicly owned area that is often devoted to trees and other greenery, it seems appropriate to call it a park. Moreover, by calling it a *park strip*, and requiring adjacent property owners to maintain it (by raking leaves, mowing grass, etc.), we are each encouraged to care for a small piece of publicly owned parkland that provides benefits to us personally as well as to the community as a whole.

In recognition of the many benefits that park strips provide, Eugene is once again requiring them in all new subdivisions. And developers and residents are required to plant the park strips with large-canopy trees, since all utility lines are now underground in these subdivisions. (Hurray!)

Even downtown, park strips are beginning to reappear in areas that have been covered with concrete for years. The recent Broadway Place development, for example, incorporates park strips along both Lincoln Street and part of Broadway. Indeed, as concern about such issues as water quality, stormwater retention, and climate change increases, we are likely to see continued expansion of park strips throughout our community. And Eugene will become an even more attractive and pleasant place for both people and trees.

(This article first appeared in the Fall 2000 edition of *ETF News*.)

MYTHS ABOUT TREE ROOTS

BEGINNING IN ELEMENTARY SCHOOL, most of us were taught that the root systems of trees are more or less mirror images of their above-ground canopies. In other words, a tree whose canopy is fifty feet tall and fifty feet wide likely has a root system fifty feet deep and fifty feet across.

Upon reflection, one quickly realizes how ridiculous this idea is. In the first place, the soil that trees grow in is seldom deeper than a few feet, and is often underlain with bedrock. And what about a 300-foot-tall coast redwood? Are its roots 300 feet deep? Hardly! Still, the myth persists.

In fact, most trees look like a brandy snifter, with a full canopy, a single and straight trunk, and a flat root system. Even on deep, fertile, and well-drained riverbottom soil—such as that which underlies much of Eugene in the vicinity of the Willamette River—most of the roots of a large bigleaf maple or Douglas-fir are in the top foot or two of soil.

Still, the idea persists—even among professional arborists—that some trees are more deeply rooted than others, and that certain tree species have deep tap roots. For example, I frequently hear arborists say that Eugene's native ponderosa (or "valley") pines have deeper roots than Douglas-firs, and are thus less prone to blowdown. In some newer developments in the south hills, where pines and firs coexist (e.g., the south end of Spring Boulevard), the firs are thus removed and the pines are left.

But on the soils in that area, which are typically only a few feet deep, neither species is more deeply rooted than the other. It is true, however, that wind passes more easily through the more open canopy of a pine than through the denser canopy of a fir, hence the fact that pines seldom go down in windstorms. The idea of pines with unusually deep roots, however, is a myth.

41

With regard to tap roots, some young trees do initially produce a major root that during the trees' first few years might, on suitable soil, grow deeper into the ground than the top grows into the sky. But that imbalance does not persist for many years. After growing relatively quickly to a depth of a few feet or more (again, on suitable soil), the tap root's growth slows to a crawl, while the rest of the root system closer to the surface begins to develop laterally. Example of trees with tap roots include some of the oaks, hickories, and Pacific madrone. None of these trees, however, develops a deep, fat, carrot-like tap root as so many of us have been led to believe.

Even on deep and well-drained soils, the root system of a typical tree is relatively shallow.

On some soils, tree roots are *unusually* shallow. For example, on the poorly drained "wetland" soils that we find in west Eugene and in the vicinity of Amazon Creek, the winter water table is at or near the surface. As a result, the roots of the relatively few tree species that can tolerate such soil conditions grow just below the surface. Even on older trees, the deepest roots may be only six inches (!) down. Since the trees on such soils are so shallowly rooted, problems with heaved sidewalks, driveways, and curbs are common because the roots of young trees develop so near the soil surface and, as they grow older and bigger, simply push up whatever is growing above them, whether it be grass or concrete.

Sweetgums (*Liquidambar styraciflua*) and pin oaks (*Quercus palustris*) are sometimes accused of having "shallow roots" and thus heaving more than their share of sidewalks and curbs. The fact is, on poorly drained soils, sweetgum and pin oak roots are no shallower than any other tree's roots. But because these two species are fairly common in our area, are well adapted to life on these soils (being native to swamps back east), and are so vigorous, we are more likely to notice the damage caused by their roots.

Unlike *trees*, the myths about tree *roots* are very deeply rooted, so these notions are unlikely to change soon. But you can help hasten a change in public opinion by explaining to others, at every opportunity, the truth about tree roots. Once they know the facts, they'll be embarrassed to admit that they ever believed in the myth!

(This article first appeared in the Summer 2003 edition of *ETF News.*)

SOILS IN EUGENE/SPRINGFIELD
AND HOW THEY AFFECT TREE GROWTH

MOST LANDOWNERS WHO RAISE CROPS—whether the crop is timber, filbert trees, strawberries, or grass seed—are familiar with the site's soil type(s) and the capability of the site for producing crop A or crop B. This is because not all soils are created equal. Some soils here in the upper Willamette Valley can grow almost anything. But most soils have some limiting characteristic that prevents them from being suitable for one crop or another.

In urban areas and elsewhere, when we are choosing what trees to plant along our streets or in our yards, we also need to be attentive to the site's soil type, to ensure that the trees we plant will thrive.

Farmers and timberland owners typically consult with soil scientists from the Soil Conservation Service (or SCS)—an agency of the U.S. Department of Agriculture. Homeowners, tree-planting organizations, and others have the right to consult with SCS staff, too, but seldom do. Instead, most people take a hit-or-miss approach. If they happen to live on a more "all-purpose" soil type, of course, anything will grow well. But if their soil is limited in any way due to its natural characteristics, there could be problems.

How Different Soils Are Distinguished

Most soils are composed of three different sizes of particles. From large to small, those particles are sand, silt, and clay. Soils with a greater percentage of large particles tend to drain well, and those in which small particles dominate are poorly drained. This makes sense, if you think about it. Say you have two small, open-ended cylinders, one filled with marbles and one filled with uncooked rice. If you pour water into the top of the cylinder containing the marbles, it moves down through the marbles quickly via the large air spaces between adjacent marbles. But water moves relatively slowly through the rice that packs together more tightly and lacks the large air spaces between the grains.

Another distinction among soils is their provenance, or where they came from and how they developed. In the Eugene-Springfield area, we happen to have three very different soil types of three distinct provenances. On the valley floor, in the vicinity of large watercourses such as the Willamette and McKenzie rivers, we find soils that came here from somewhere else—mostly the West Cascades—during past floods. These soils are somewhat variable, but for the most part they are deep and well-drained. (On scattered sites with a lot of sand or river cobble, however, the soil is excessively drained or "droughty" because there aren't enough *small* soil particles to keep water from flowing right down through the soil to the water table.)

Most of the soil on the hills developed on-site from the weathering of the bedrock that underlies the site. Some of the hill soils in our area are weathered basalt—e.g., Skinner Butte in downtown Eugene. Others are weathered sedimentary rock that formed from ancient marine sediments laid down when the land here was beneath the Pacific Ocean. Soils on the hills are relatively shallow—you don't have to dig down very far before hitting bedrock—and fairly well-drained, due in part to the sloping topography of the hills themselves.

The third general soil type we find in this area consists largely of volcanic ash that fell from the sky some 7,700 years ago during eruptions of Mt. Mazama, the enormous volcano whose collapsed remains form Crater Lake. The volcanic ash presumably covered most of this area for decades or centuries following the volcano's final eruptions, but over time, it eroded off the surrounding hills. On most of the valley floor, it was moved out of the area (or perhaps covered by different soil) by extensive flooding of local rivers that has occurred during the millennia since the eruptions.

Soils derived from volcanic ash are found primarily at the bases or toe-slopes of hills—in a doughnut-like ring around the lower slopes of Skinner Butte, for example—and in basins within or near the hills that have been unaffected by the flooding of the Willamette River, such as the Amazon Park area in Eugene. Additionally, there is a large area of this soil type in west Eugene, bounded roughly by Highway 126 on the south and Greenhill Road on the west.

Because this type of soil is composed of such small airborne particles, it is very poorly drained. Most years, it is waterlogged from November through May or June, with standing water in many places. During the summer drought, the soil turns brick-hard and develops broad cracks in it, as the clay-like particles have what is called a high shrink-swell capacity.

In our area, although undisturbed soils of this type support a rich and diverse plant and animal community, they are much maligned by gardeners, as most of the plants that we humans like to cultivate—from petunias and tomatoes, to rhododendrons and maple trees—are native to better drained soils and languish or die when planted in poorly drained soils. But these soils are not "bad"; they are simply poorly drained.

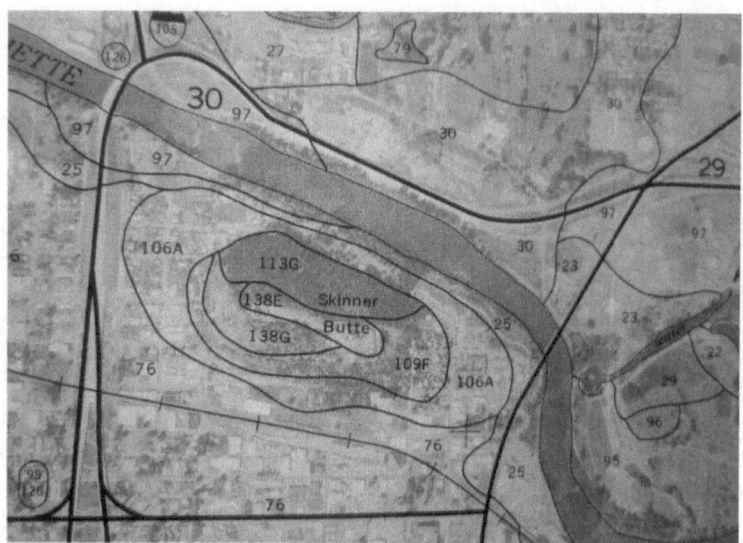

Close-up of the SCS's detailed soil map for downtown Eugene, showing the "doughnut" of poorly drained soil (106A) around the base of Skinner Butte.

Soil Classification

In their Soil Survey of Lane County (1987), soil scientists with the SCS identify more than a hundred different soil types. Even their map of "*general soil types*" still has 22 different soils listed.

In an effort to simplify soil classification and make the information more accessible to the general public in the Eugene-Springfield area, I developed in the 1990s a system composed of just three major soil types or classes, as outlined above. Because the SCS uses Roman numerals to designate eight different "capability classes"—which indicate the suitability of soils for the cultivation of field crops (Class I soils having few limitations to restrict their use and Class VIII having so many limitations as to nearly preclude their use for commercial crop production)—I elected to use capital letters to designate the different soil classes. So Class A soils are "river soils"; Class B soils are "hill soils"; and Class C soils are "wetland soils" (see chart).

Class A Soils

Since most of the first Euro-American settlers here in the upper Willamette Valley in the mid-1800s were farmers—who settled on the best soils for the cultivation of crops—the downtowns and older neighborhoods of both Eugene and Springfield sit atop some of the best soil in North America: deep, fertile, well-drained Class A soil known to soil scientists as Malabon Silt Loam. Even during the wettest periods of the winter, one seldom sees standing water on these sites.

Good places to see the natural biotic communities supported by such soils include the Alton Baker Park woodlands north of the Autzen/Frohnmayer footbridge in Eugene and the woodlands at Dorris Ranch in Springfield. An upper canopy of bigleaf maple, Douglas-fir, and grand fir—sometimes single-species woodlands, sometimes mixed—shades a rich understory of deciduous shrubs such as Indian–plum and vine maple, plus herbaceous plants or "wildflowers."

On sites within this zone that are *excessively* drained due to the presence of a lot of river cobble and/or sand, more drought-tolerant native trees such as incense-cedar, valley ponderosa pine, madrone, and Oregon white oak predominate, and the understory is less lush than on loamier soils.

Class B Soils

On hill soils, conifer forests predominate these days—largely of Douglas-fir, but sometimes including valley ponderosa pine, grand fir, and incense-cedar. But before 1850 and the cessation of annual burning of the local landscape by area aborigines, a savanna landscape of widely scattered oaks (both Oregon white and California black) and a few conifers cloaked these hills. These days, shrubs in the forest undercanopy are mostly western hazel, vine maple, and low Oregon-grape. Sword ferns and herbaceous plants such as white trillium and vancouveria are, in places, quite common.

Good examples of largely pristine Class B or hill soils include the forested part of Hendricks Park, most of Masonic Cemetery, and Spencer Butte Park.

Class C Soils

Most Class C or wetland soils were largely treeless before 1850—due once again to the frequent human-set fires that swept across the valley floor and up into the surrounding hills. But in the absence of those fires, trees moved in on many sites—mostly Oregon ash and Douglas hawthorn, with occasional valley ponderosa pine and Oregon white oak in areas that are slightly less waterlogged in winter.

Local examples of woodlands on Class C soils include the ash groves at Amazon Park, and the Willow Creek Nature Conservancy site near 18th and Bertelsen.

SOIL CLASSES OF EUGENE-SPRINGFIELD			
	Class A River Soil	Class B Hill Soil	Class C Wetland Soil
Provenance	Flood-borne and mostly from the West Cascades	Weathering of sub-surface bedrock	Airborne ash from Mt. Mazama eruptions
Characteristics	Deep, fertile, well drained loam (in most places); moles common	Relatively shallow and fairly well drained (due in part to topography)	Poorly drained, with standing water common in winter; dry, cracked, and brick-hard in summer; moles absent
Signature native trees broad-leafed trees conifers	bigleaf maple Douglas-fir	Oregon white oak Douglas-fir	Oregon ash valley ponderosa pine

Determining Soil Type

Once one is familiar with the three major soil classes in this area—A, B, and C—it is easy to determine soil type simply by looking at a neighborhood's existing trees. If you're on or near the valley floor, and the site supports an abundance of large, luxuriant trees—especially bigleaf maple and Douglas-fir—and you seldom see the roots of street-side trees pushing up curbs or sidewalks, then you're on Class A or river soil. (Of course, if you're visiting in midwinter and see no standing water anywhere, that's a good sign, too!)

When on or near the valley floor where Douglas-firs and bigleaf maples are conspicuously absent or growing very poorly—and the roots of many trees are at or near the surface and pushing up sidewalks, curbs, and driveways—you're on Class C or wetland soil. In mid-winter, lawns in these areas are squishy and often have pools of standing water.

And, of course, if you're on a hilly site, well . . . that's easy: it must be Class B or hill soil. Unless grades have been changed due to construction or the soil has been compacted by heavy machinery, you should never see standing water in these areas.

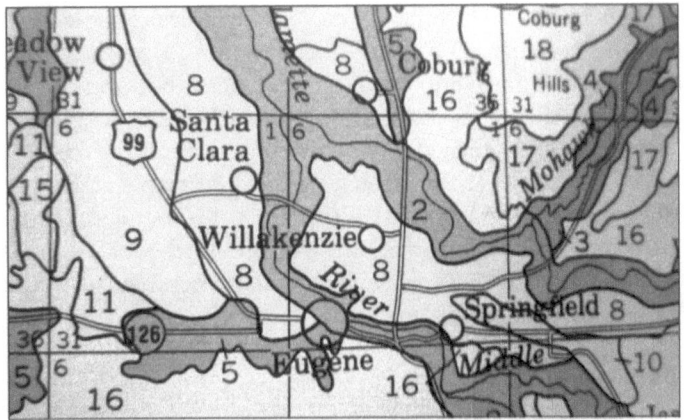

A close-up of the Soil Conservation Service's "General Soil Map" showing river soils (2, 8, and 9) hill soils (16, 17, and 18), and wetland soils (5).

Choosing Trees Based on Soil Type

When it comes to choosing trees for the three different soil types, you can be confident that pretty much any tree—both native and non-native—will thrive on Class A soils, except in pockets where the soil is excessively drained, or in linear post-flood drainage channels where poorly-drained clay is found.

On Class B soils, limiting factors are soil depth—since bedrock is sometimes very near the surface—and droughtiness in the summer, especially on south-facing slopes. Most trees, both native and non-native, will thrive here, especially if provided with supplemental irrigation. But if summer water is not available, you need to shrink your palette of suitable trees somewhat and focus more on native trees, or non-native trees that come from regions that, like ours, have a summer drought.

Class C soils are the most limiting when it comes to tree growth. On non-irrigated sites, trees must withstand both the waterlogged soils of winter as well as the concrete-like soils of summer, after the soil has dried out. And one must understand and accept that the roots of every tree on these soils will be right at the surface, so there are sure to be problems if we (ahem!) place our concrete and asphalt too close to them. Also, it's not worth amending these soils to make them better suited for a larger variety of trees. For an "upland" tree to be able to mature on Class C or "lowland" soils would require countless cubic yards of soil and/or a drainage system. It's more sensible to choose a tree that is appropriate for Class C soils, rather than try to "improve" the soil. Again, nothing is "wrong" with these soils; they are simply poorly drained.

Since Class C soils are the most limiting for tree growth, the list of appropriate species is necessarily short. Very few trees can tolerate both the winter-wet and summer-dry nature of these soils. Oregon ash, green ash, pin oak, and sweetgum are some of the best; but tupelo, European hornbeam, London plane, elms, and red horse-chestnuts are fairly tolerant, too. If one is able to provide some summer irrigation, the list can be expanded to include other (non-native) ashes, red maple, and catalpa. The only native conifer suited to Class C soils is valley ponderosa pine. Non-native conifers—that will thrive only if provided with some summer water—include most spruces, as well as bald-cypress and dawn redwood, both of which are deciduous.

A Final Note

With a little practice, anyone can learn to distinguish the three different soil classes in the Eugene-Springfield area, just by looking at a site's topography, its apparent drainage, and the existing vegetation in the vicinity. But be aware that changes in grade, construction practices that are abusive to native soils, and outright removal of soil and "replacement" with rock or rubble all will affect future tree growth. If in doubt about a soil's class or its condition, it's always best to be on the safe side by choosing a tree from the "short list" of trees suitable for Class C soils.

(This article first appeared in the Spring 2013 newsletter of *Friends of Trees*.)

CALIFORNIA BUCKEYE: A HARBINGER OF SUMMER

ONE OF THE MORE SPECTACULAR flowering trees that can be grown in our area is the California buckeye (*Aesculus californica*), a close relative of the common European horsechestnut (*Aesculus hippocastanum*) that blooms here in April and May.

For most of the year, the buckeye's green canopy goes largely unnoticed, but when the tree is in full bloom in June, you can't miss it with its long clusters of sweetly scented white flowers.

Although rarely planted locally—and virtually unavailable in nurseries—this species deserves more attention. A native of California's Coast Range and the Sierra foothills, where it typically grows as a gawky shrub or small tree, it develops under cultivation into a pretty and symmetrical little tree. A superb, two-trunked specimen grows near the southeast corner of East 15th Avenue and Walnut Street in the Fairmount Neighborhood. Although planted in the backyard, its canopy is fully visible from the street. [*Author note in 2019: The tree has been removed since this article's publication in 2009.*]

The California buckeye should grow well most anywhere in Eugene, including areas with poorly drained soils such as the lower parts of the Amazon Neighborhood east of Amazon Park—where another tree of this species grows behind a house in the 2500 block of Kincaid Street. Because of its relatively small stature and spreading canopy, it also deserves consideration as a street-side tree, even where there are overhead electrical distribution lines. The tree is drought-tolerant, cold-hardy, and an absolute knockout during the first few weeks of summer!

(Please turn the page to see a photograph of California buckeye in bloom.)

Close-up of California buckeye inflorescence (flower cluster).

(This article first appeared in the Summer 2009 edition of *ETF News.*)

IRVINGTON DRIVE RESIDENTS
TO GET STREET TREES

THESE DAYS ANY NEW OR RECONSTRUCTED STREET in Eugene must include park strips planted with trees. That is, unless the construction is on a *county* or *state* road within the city limits.

Last summer, the Lane County Department of Public Works proposed improvements to Irvington Drive in the Santa Clara area. The road is a county road, and county engineers declared that the improvements would mean widening the two-lane roadway to three lanes for motorized vehicles, as well as bike lanes and curbside sidewalks, thus filling the entire 60-foot right-of-way with asphalt and concrete.

However, at a meeting of interested local parties, including traffic engineers, ETF board member Whitey Lueck, a surprise guest, made his own proposal: A *two*-lane street lined with large-canopy trees and setback sidewalks, creating a pleasant street for pedestrians, bicyclists, and drivers.

Many of the stakeholders in attendance were neighbors and residents of Irvington Drive and were very pleased to hear of this new proposal. They advised county staff to include the park strips in the design in an effort to bring more trees and greenery into what would otherwise be a bleak and lifeless roadway. County staff agreed, and so a new design was to be considered.

However, the county's oversight advisory group—called the Roads Advisory Committee (RAC)—voted to overturn the staff's new proposal and supported instead the original plan which resembled an airport runway more than a pleasant street.

Irvington Drive residents Vince LaRochelle and Millie Redford, among others, were not ready to give in to this latest turn of events. The neighbors established a grassroots campaign to reverse the RAC decision.

Vince, Millie, and other neighbors visited *every* homeowner along Irvington Drive to discuss their concerns about the proposed roadway improvements.

As a result, almost half (!) of Irvington property owners wrote to the county Public Works Department requesting a special public hearing before the Board of County Commissioners. The hearing was granted, and more than twenty residents spoke in support of a *narrower* road with room for park strips and trees. After listening to their testimony, the county commissioners saw the wisdom of this design and voted in favor of the trees.

This Triumph-for-Trees—and for livability in general—underscores the importance of citizen involvement in public works projects, and the need to follow those projects through to completion. Construction work on Irvington Drive begins this summer, and decisions still to be made include tree species selection and choice of groundcovers. ETF will be watching closely.

(This article first appeared in the Spring 2002 edition of *ETF News*.)

BUILDING COMMUNITY BY
WORKING TOGETHER

MOST OF THE PROJECTS that Eugene Tree Foundation works on in our community are accomplished with the help of City of Eugene staff and resources, whether we're planting new streetside trees in a neighborhood or advocating for increased tree protection during construction and development. This amicable partnership has existed for as long as ETF has been around—which is more than ten years now—and benefits all of us in myriad ways.

During the planning for a tree planting, for example, ETF volunteers contact adjacent property owners to apprise them of the upcoming project. Property owners tend to respond more favorably to ideas coming from a small community group than they would if those same ideas were proposed by The City—a huge organization that for some people can be somewhat imposing.

ETF workers also call in the "utility locates" to ensure that our shovels don't hit underground irrigation lines or electrical conduits on planting day, and we advertise the planting so that help will be available to get the trees in the ground. But it's the City of Eugene that provides the trees through the NeighborWoods program and provides the shovels and gloves and porta-potty and so much more when planting day finally arrives. And in ETF's Trees-for-Concrete projects, City crews provide the machinery and staff to do the heavy work that would be impossible—or inordinately expensive—for our little non-profit group to do on its own.

By working together, City of Eugene staff and ETF volunteers accomplish much more than if we were working alone on the same projects. Each organization does what it does best and draws on the resources available to it—people, money, equipment—that will get the job done in the most efficient manner.

Working side by side with City staff, ETF volunteers learn about the jobs that staff do and find out that they are just as devoted as we are to trees and to making our community a more livable place. Friendships develop that persist long after a particular project is finished. The more we learn about "them," the more likely we are to support "their" programs by providing testimony, for example, during a Budget Committee meeting. And the more they get to know *us*, the more likely they are to respond positively to our occasional requests for assistance.

Isn't this the way that all communities should work? After all, a *community* is by definition "the people with *common* interests living in a particular area." These days, many people refer to large public organizations and private corporations as "they," which makes those entities seem distant and intractable. But once we realize that we're all part of the same community and begin to use the pronoun "we" instead of "they," it makes working together and accomplishing great things so much easier.

Tree-planting volunteers at a recent Campus Re-Leaf project near the University of Oregon.

(This article first appeared in the Summer 2007 edition of *ETF News*.)

WHEN RAKING UP IS HARD TO DO—
WHY NOT LET LYING LEAVES LIE?

THE YOUNG WOMAN'S COMMENT still rings in my ears. It was the middle of summer, and she and her family had just moved into a new house right next to a little maple woods. I'd stopped by to say hello and during our conversation, I noticed that all the ground in the woods had been very recently raked clean; in fact, it looked as if it had been vacuumed.

When I asked her about it, she said, "Oh, you would not believe what a MESS it was here in the woods when we moved in—there were still leaves lying on the ground from last fall!" I was at a loss for words. All I could think of were questions. Why had I never thought of raking leaves in a woods? What did this apparently very conscientious homeowner think she might accomplish by doing this? How does she feel about the many thousands of square miles of wild forests in our state that have not yet had the opportunity to have *their* leaves raked up?

I couldn't pass up the chance to enlighten my neighbor about the wonders of leaf mulch. In the course of our brief conversation, she seemed to be an understanding person who just might be swayed by new information. She would probably, at the very least, consider different ideas and not reject them simply because they were at odds with what she already believed. So I took a deep breath and crossed my fingers.

I stared briefly at the leafless forest floor, then back at her, and I winced a wee bit. I said something about how weeds just love to move in onto bare soil. A natural leaf mulch, however, is one of the most effective "herbicides" because leaves shade the ground, preventing most weed seeds from germinating. She nodded approvingly.

Then I asked her if she thought that recycling was a good idea. Oh, yes, I was assured, she and her family were avid recyclers. So I explained how leaf fall is just nature's way of recycling nutrients and organic matter. And by removing the leaves, we interrupt a very important cycle and can thereby cause a variety of problems. For one, the health of our plants may slowly decline, unless, of course, we artificially replace the nutrients and organic matter lost by removing the leaves. And why spend the time and labor replacing those things, when you can avoid the problem altogether by letting leaves stay put in the first place?

Second, leaf litter, whether it's in a wild forest or in your own backyard, plays a variety of important ecological roles. Like any good mulch, it helps moderate soil temperatures and conserves soil moisture, which benefits your plants in many ways. And an adequate layer of constantly decomposing leaf litter supports myriad other life forms, too, from centipedes to towhees, which together help maintain the health of the woods or your yard.

Third, leaf litter reduces the impact of heavy winter rains that can compact the soil. The leaves act as a sponge to absorb rainfall, then let it pass more slowly into the soil instead of running off. And when compaction and runoff are prevented, less precious soil erodes off into our streams and rivers.

So far, so good. Now for the hard part: aesthetics. I asked her if she and her family like to visit the national forests. They do. And did she think they looked "messy" with so many leaves and twigs lying on the ground? "Well, not really . . . but what are you getting at?" I simply wanted to know if her idea of "pretty" depended on whether the landscape was an urban one or a rural one. And if it did, then why the different standards? She said she'd have to think about that one.

She then asked me, "But what about the leaves that land on my lawn?" And I explained that, yes, leaves could, of course, kill a lawn if left there very long. But those leaves could be raked into shrub beds or onto the vegetable garden for the winter. And maybe, instead of trying to have lawn under or near trees, she could just plant shrubs there and let the leaves filter down through the shrubs to the ground. Talk about low-maintenance landscaping!

I hardly expected to instantly convert my conversant. But by the time I left, I had the good feeling that the points I had been allowed to make had not fallen on deaf ears. The big test, though, will come in the next few weeks. As the leaves begin to fall, I'm hoping that at least one other person will be looking at them in a different way—not as "work to be done" but as wonders of nature that do so very much for us, and for free.

(This article first appeared in the 7 October 1995 edition of *Lane Living*.)

FRUIT TREES CAN BE ESPALIERED

L ATE WINTER IS A CHOICE TIME here in the upper Willamette Valley for planting trees. Some broad-leafed, deciduous trees (e.g., maples and oaks) can now be purchased *bare root*. Because their roots are not surrounded by a heavy ball of soil, bare-root trees are easier and less expensive for nurseries to ship and far easier for the purchaser to handle. Plus, the use of bare-root trees is more environmentally friendly because most of the soil that the young trees grew in stays in the nursery and the trees' lighter shipping weight requires less fossil fuel to get them to their destination.

When most of us think of trees, we think of pleasant shade, beautiful leaves, and even flowers. But let's not forget the broad-leafed, deciduous trees that bear edible *fruits*. Although many of the older homes in our area have fruit trees in their yards, such trees are conspicuously absent from the landscapes of most new homes. We can change that.

A great variety of fruit trees is available in local garden centers. The bare-root trees are usually displayed either in large bins of moist sawdust or in tightly sealed plastic tubes that prevent the tree's roots and the bark or sawdust surrounding them from drying out.

Most named *cultivars* (short for *cul*-tivated *var*-ieties) such as 'Bartlett' pear and 'Granny Smith' apple are grafted onto what are called dwarfing rootstocks, which reduce the eventual size of the tree. Standard apple trees, for example, can grow nearly forty feet tall. These days, many commercial growers and most homeowners prefer plants that are grafted onto dwarf (or semi-dwarf) rootstocks because the trees are easier to work with and they begin to bear at a younger age. Be mindful, though, that unlike other broad-leafed, deciduous trees, fruit trees need to be pruned every winter. Even an apple on dwarf rootstock can, in the absence of annual pruning, quickly reach fifteen feet or more in height. But with regular pruning, such a tree can easily be kept under six to eight feet in height.

My favorite way to train and care for fruit trees in the home landscape is to *espalier* (ess-PAH-lee-ay or ess-PAL-yer) them. The first time I saw espaliered fruit trees in Europe, I thought, "I can't do that! It must be incredibly difficult!" It's not. Indeed, I find espaliered trees far easier to look after than conventional, open-grown trees. In France, espalier refers to the brick or stone wall against which fruit trees are sometimes grown. Originally, this was done to permit the cultivation of fruit trees that were not quite hardy in the region by providing a more protected, warmer microclimate. These days, though, people espalier fruit trees so the trees take up less space in small gardens, so the fruit is more accessible, or just for artistic reasons.

In our area, I prefer to grow espaliered trees out in the open garden rather than against a wall. The microclimate provided by south-facing walls, in particular, can make trees bloom too early, so the flowers risk getting caught in a late frost. (If you choose to espalier a fruit tree against a building, east- and west-facing walls are the safest spots.) I train my trees' main branches along stout wires or against a fence. Although there are many fancy ways to espalier young fruit trees, I prefer to simply train the tree's two lowest branches left and right along the first wire (about two to three feet above the ground). Then along a second wire two to three feet above the first, I train two more young branches, one to the left and one to the right. You can, of course, go for a third or even a fourth level.

Because I choose not to use any pesticides on my fruit trees, some fruits can in some years be "blemished," but that doesn't affect their taste. And by growing several different kinds of fruit trees—or different cultivars of a single fruit—you help ensure that, good year or bad, you'll still be certain to have plenty of fresh fruit of one kind or another.

So if you're thinking about planting any trees this spring, consider planting fruit-bearing trees. Whether open grown or espaliered, they provide all the benefits that any tree provides, plus an abundance of fresh fruit for you, your family, and your friends. In addition to traditional tree fruits like apple and cherry, you might also consider some of the more exotic fruits such as Asian pear, oriental persimmon, and the simply delicious pawpaw from eastern North America.

As much fun as some of us dendrophiles (tree-lovers) have raking leaves in fall, it's even more enjoyable to rake in all the delicious produce that fruit-bearing trees provide, at very low cost.

(This article first appeared in the 2 March 1998 edition of
The Springfield News.)

COAST REDWOODS BUSY IN MID-WINTER

ALTHOUGH MOST TREES IN OUR AREA are dormant during the winter, a number of evergreen conifers are now engaged in "reproductive activities." The action peaks for the coast redwood (*Sequoia sempervirens*) in January.

Like almost all other conifers, redwoods are *monoecious* (pronounced moh-NEE-shuss, from the Greek words for "one house"). This means that the tree's reproductive structures or "cones" are unisexual—male *or* female, but not *both* sexes in the same structure—yet both the male and female cones live in the same "house" or tree. (In *dioecious* or "two-house" conifers such as yews, the sexes occur on separate trees.)

Since late fall, the pollen-bearing (male) cones have become increasingly visible at the tips of branchlets in the redwood's lower canopy. The future seed-bearing (female) cones—which will receive the ripe pollen—are much more difficult to discern right now, but by early spring they will become more conspicuous.

During occasional dry and mild periods, local redwoods can be seen releasing clouds of their yellowish pollen into the air. After pollination is completed, the pollen cones will dry up and in time be shed, while the seed cones will increase in girth as the seeds develop within them, and eventually reach the size of marbles. Then in late fall, the cones will open, dispersing their tiny seeds to the wind.

You can see large redwoods at the northeast and northwest corners of 12th and Washington, as well as nearby at the southwest corner of 10th and Lawrence. And, of course, there's a lovely, two-trunked one with very low hanging branches by the sidewalk in front of my house. Like most redwoods, it just adores having visitors!

(Please turn the page to see a photograph of coast redwood pollen cones.)

Ripe pollen cones at the tips of two coast redwood branchlets.

(This article first appeared in the Winter 2007 edition of *ETF News.*)

THE TREES OF THE
EUGENE PIONEER CEMETERY

O NE OF THE ASPECTS of the Eugene Pioneer Cemetery that appeals most to the casual visitor is its landscape dominated by large conifers. Few visitors, however, are aware of the site's landscape history, and how dramatically it has changed since the cemetery's inception in 1872.

At that time, not a single tree stood on the present site. And it's not because all of the trees that had once grown there were cut down by early settlers. Rather, this site—like most of present-day Eugene—had been treeless for millennia due to the cultural practices of the area's aborigines who set fire to the valley floor on a regular basis, thus largely preventing trees from getting established.

Although the cemetery site itself was originally treeless, a visitor could have seen trees in the distance, as the banks of the Willamette River were heavily wooded with maple, cottonwood, alder, and Douglas-fir. And on the nearby hillsides, widely spaced oaks—both Oregon white and California black—could be seen, as well as scattered conifers including valley ponderosa pine and Douglas-fir.

It's hard to imagine these days, but the view from the early cemetery must have been magnificent, since there were no trees to impede it! From the grass- and wildflower-covered mound, one could see from what we now call the South Hills, all the way to the Coast Range in the west. Skinner Butte lay just a mile or so away. And less than ten miles to the northeast, rising abruptly from the valley floor, were the relatively lofty summits of the Coburg Hills.

One of the first tasks that cemetery caretakers had was getting trees established. Most of the trees that local nurseries at that time raised were fruit- and nut-bearing trees that provided food. And more exotic trees, even if they were available, required a degree of care and summer watering that likely was unavailable. So all of the trees in the initial plantings were local conifers which were adapted, of course, to our area's summer drought, and were readily available and easy to transplant. Perhaps, too, conifers were chosen because of their more stately or formal form or silhouette.

Douglas-firs (left and right sides of photo) and incense-cedars (center) line a cemetery path in 2013.

Broad-leafed trees such as oaks and maples were apparently not part of the early plantings or, if they were, they failed to get established. The native oaks are relatively difficult to transplant, and our lovely native bigleaf maples, although easy to transplant, would have had difficulty getting established on the more droughty "hill soils" such as those at the cemetery, unlike the deep, fertile river loam of downtown Eugene, where the maples thrived and were very popular.

The first aerial photograph of the cemetery site was taken in 1936 and shows clearly the formal design of the early plantings. Rows of conifers—mostly Douglas-firs, but also quite a few incense-cedars—in the shape of a perfect square outlined the northern part of the current cemetery. And *double* rows of conifers marched toward the center of the square from the midpoint of each of the square's sides. These double rows or *allées* of trees terminated just before reaching the open area in the square's center.

Later plantings began to fill in other parts of the initial square and extended somewhat toward the south*west* portion of the site. Interestingly, the south*east* part of the cemetery remained largely treeless until fairly recently.

These days, conifers still dominate the site—with most of them, of course, well over a century old—but a few broad-leafed trees have moved in on their own, as well. They include bigleaf maples, English oaks (probably brought in by scrub jays from the oaks in Memorial Quad north of the Knight Library), madrones, a lovely eastern black walnut in the cemetery's southwest sector, and even a single Oregon white oak near the intersection of 18th and Potter.

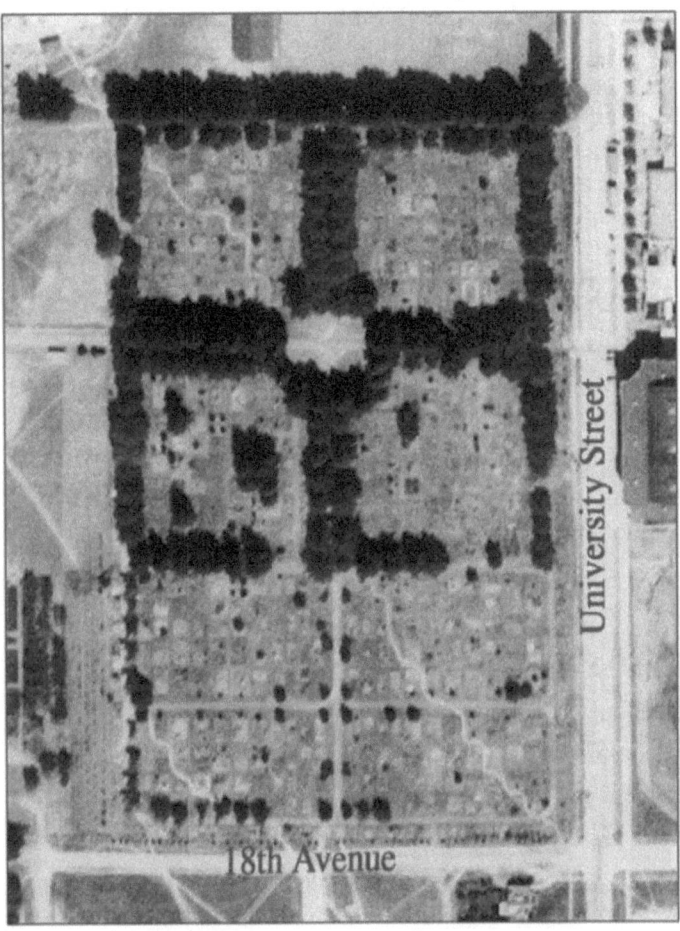

Aerial view of the Pioneer Cemetery—north at top—in 1936.

Across the United States, many cemeteries halted tree plantings years ago, because trees, beautiful as they were, had come to be seen as liabilities. There were always leaves to rake—in cemeteries where broad-leafed trees dominated—and fallen branches to remove. In addition, there was occasional storm cleanup and removal of trees that had died. With increasingly limited budgets, trees were one of the first amenities to be axed, so to speak. These days, it's all some cemeteries can do just to mow the grass.

But because a single powerful storm could fell dozens of the Eugene Pioneer Cemetery's older trees, it is essential that the next generation of trees be already in the ground and growing, to help ensure that the cemetery will always provide a canopy which can provide both shade and beauty for visitors, as well as habitat for the many birds, beneficial insects, and other wildlife that call the cemetery home.

So it's heartening to see that a dozen or so Douglas-firs have been planted within the past decade in the southeastern part of the site, so Oregon's state tree is likely to continue to grace the cemetery grounds for many decades to come. In planning for the future, the cemetery might also consider putting together a management plan for its tree canopy, which would outline the ongoing care of existing trees, as well as how new trees will be incorporated during the coming decades.

This recently planted Douglas-fir helps to ensure that the cemetery's tree canopy will be maintained well into the future.

(This article first appeared in the Summer 2013 newsletter of *Friends of Trees*.)

IF A TREE FALLS IN THE WOODS,
TAKE IT HOME

EVERY DECEMBER, when I start to think of the pretty little tree covered with lights that will grace my front window for a few weeks, I first go out to the garage to be sure that my handsaw is both sharp and ready for its annual trip to the woods. Having grown up on the Eastern Seaboard, where conifers (cone-bearing trees) are a real rarity in the woods, I truly love going out into the snowy Cascades to look for what will be, for me, the perfect tree.

Some of my friends think that my behavior at this season smacks of cruelty. How can such a phytophilic (or "plant-loving" in Greek) guy as I am feel so gleeful about taking a plant's life? Well, I eat carrots, too. And how unfair, it seems to me, to suggest that a young fir tree's life is any more important, or more worthy of saving, than the carrot's life. How do you think that makes the carrot feel?

The fact is, I try to respect all life. And by carefully removing a single young conifer from a stand of many young conifers, I know that empty space will quickly be filled by other young trees nearby that will need more space as they grow older. Nature just works like that.

Conifers grow here in the Pacific Northwest in greater abundance and variety than anywhere else in the world. Why? It's the climate. Conifers are ideally suited to our winter-wet, summer-dry climate, doing most of their photosynthesis and growing during the mild and moist months from October to June, and then mostly shutting down during the summer and early fall to conserve water. Even in the middle of winter, as long as temperatures are above freezing, conifers are working hard to make the world a better place, happily converting carbon dioxide and water, in the presence of light, into carbohydrates and oxygen.

So how does one decide where to look for a tree here in the Land of Many Conifers? The best place is on nearby national forest land. By purchasing an inexpensive permit, available at district ranger stations, you may then cut however many trees you paid for. It's as easy as that. And compared to the number of mature trees, fish, elk, mushrooms, and everything else taken from these same forest lands every year, removing one or two young trees makes a relatively small mark.

And what kind of tree does one look for? Douglas-fir (*Pseudotsuga menziesii*) and grand fir (*Abies grandis*) grow at elevations below about 3,500 feet and are eminently suited to being indoors for a few weeks. At middle elevations (3,500 to 4,500 feet or so) grows the much-sought noble fir (*Abies procera*). And at higher elevations still can be found the subalpine fir (*Abies lasiocarpa*), the distinctive and almost spire-like conifer of the high country.

Make your trip to the woods an all-day outing, taking along plenty of warm clothes and enough food to keep everyone happy until you return home in the late afternoon. In addition to just looking for and cutting down a tree, spend some time skiing or snowshoeing in the vicinity (if you're up in the snow zone) or taking a hike if at lower elevations.

Then get that tree home, make a fresh cut at the base, put it in its stand that you'll fill with water, and place it in one of the cooler parts of the room instead of right next to a south window or next to a radiator. The cooler the spot, the longer your tree will last.

When you go out to find your tree, try not to make the mistake I made about ten years ago. A friend and I decided to ski several miles up a snow-covered forest road to reach the noble-fir zone. It was a delightfully sunny day without any wind, so we could sit shirtless and enjoy our lunches while looking out across the winter landscape. After cutting our "perfect" noble fir, we attached a rope to its trunk and, in Christmas-card style, skied back down the trail.

By late in the afternoon, however, the snow had developed a crust. So by the time we reached the car and lifted the tree up out of the snow, we discovered to our chagrin that the entire bottom side of the tree had been scraped free of needles and bark! As we were not about to ski back up the hill that late in the day, we settled instead for a nice little Douglas-fir we found nearby and bade a fond farewell to the noble fir we'd so unintentionally mistreated.

After the holidays, consider putting your tree to work in the landscape around your house or apartment. It can serve as a winter refuge for birds by just laying it on the ground in a protected area or by tying it up to a post. Or you might choose to just remove all the branches and lay them over your perennial beds for decoration as well as winter protection; the trunk can just be put out of sight in the back of an established shrub bed, where it eventually will rot. I personally prefer these gentle options, instead of seeing the tree tossed into the back of a truck or turned noisily into a pile of chips and tinsel.

Finally, if you choose to purchase a potted (living) tree, be sure that the site where you plan to plant it will provide enough room for the tree to grow comfortably into adulthood. And be careful not to keep it inside too long or in too warm a room, as it could "break bud" and begin growing. Above all, just enjoy this wonderful season and all the sights and scents of conifers, wherever you are.

(This article first appeared in the 6 December 1996 edition of
Northeast Neighbor.)

TREES AND OVERHEAD UTILITY WIRES

THE WIRES STRUNG BETWEEN UTILITY POLES along Eugene's streets and alleys are a mystery to most people, as well as a considerable obstacle to many of our community's trees. Only some of the wires we see are "electrical distribution" lines. Generally, they are the three (or sometimes two) wires atop the crossbar at the very top of the pole. The rest of the wires attached lower on the pole are for cable television, telephone, internet, and so forth.

For safety reasons, federal law requires a certain number of feet of clearance from electric lines, depending on the voltage they're carrying. The higher the voltage, the greater the clearance required. But the rest of the wires can sail right through the tree canopy and even touch a tree's trunk without posing a significant safety hazard.

Most of the trees planted in the public right-of-way—typically between curb and sidewalk in areas with setback sidewalks—are cared for by the City of Eugene's tree crews, who know better than to "top," butcher, or otherwise abuse our trees. However, our local electric utility (Eugene Water and Electric Board) is responsible for the pruning of all trees in the public right-of-way that grow beneath or near electric lines. What EWEB and its contractors do to trees is seldom very pretty. An effort has been made in recent years to improve tree pruning practices near electric lines, but there isn't much one can do for a tree that's been mutilated for decades.

Since about 1970, utility lines in all new developments in Eugene have been placed underground, providing aesthetic benefits as well as permitting large-canopy trees to develop unhindered in the publicly owned park strips. And, whenever money is available, EWEB and the City of Eugene are placing existing overhead lines underground. (An example is along Franklin Boulevard between Agate Street and Onyx where, during the upcoming Bus

Rapid Transit construction, the wires on the north side of Franklin will be buried.)

Where older trees have been mutilated repeatedly over the years, the best solution is often to give the trees a big hug for their persistence, cut them down, and replant. For example, along Adams Street between Third and Sixth avenues, where the wires have recently been put underground, the sad, old trees filled with rot need to be replaced now with new, large-canopy trees.

But there are other options. In parts of the United States, for example, electric wires are sometimes strung on crossbars attached directly to the tree trunks of older street-side trees (Figure A). No need for poison-impregnated utility poles!

Figure A

In some of Portland's older neighborhoods and elsewhere in the United States, the electric lines are heavily insulated and bundled together into a single wire which then passes either through the tree's canopy or is attached to a shorter-than-average pole beneath the canopies of larger trees (Figure B).

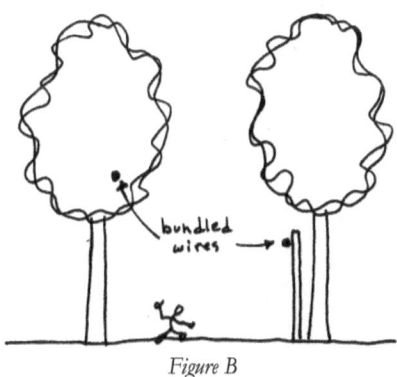

Figure B

Sometimes, where trees and utility poles are offset, simply moving the wires a few feet to one side or the other (from, say, a typical T-configuration to what is called an *alley arm*) will permit trees to get up and above the wires and out of the way. This would be an ideal solution for the repeatedly butchered sweetgums along the south side of East 19th Avenue in front of South Eugene High School (Figure C).

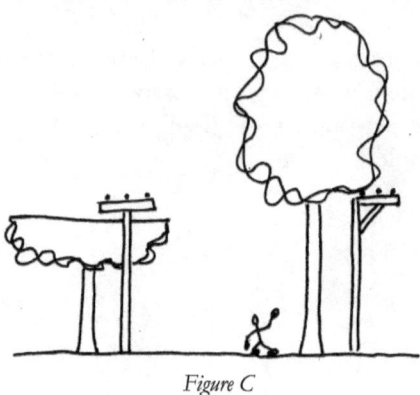

Figure C

These simple and inexpensive compromises between conventional overhead wires (and butchered trees) and buried wires merit consideration locally. EWEB would no longer have to pay for frequent pruning of the trees, and that savings could be passed on to ratepayers. And we'd all benefit by having healthier and larger-canopied trees along our streets.

(This article first appeared in the Fall 2003 edition of *ETF News*.)

THEY MAY BE CUTE, BUT SQUIRRELS
CAN BE A PAIN

WHEN FRIENDS FROM FRANCE VISITED last spring, they couldn't get over the abundance of squirrels in the Springfield-Eugene area. It seemed like everywhere we went, they were aiming their video camera at the furry critters. I was quite amused by it all.

In France, squirrels are seldom seen in urban areas, and even in rural areas they are a relatively uncommon sight. But here in the United States, they are of course a part of most every park, college campus, and backyard from Philadelphia to San Francisco. And, depending on your perspective, they are either a delightful part of the landscape or a nuisance that might just as well be eliminated.

As a gardener, I have somewhat mixed feelings about squirrels. My former suburban house sat amid the remains of a walnut and filbert orchard, and there were squirrels galore. And because my yard was one of very few in the neighborhood that was dog free, the squirrels preferred to bury their nuts in my vegetable beds, in my lawn, and pretty much everywhere else. I grew accustomed to the little holes they left behind in winter and spring after they dug up their nuts to eat, and the many walnut and filbert seedlings that developed from "forgotten" nuts.

For a while, though, the squirrels did commandeer my bird feeder which annoyed me mostly in a financial way. But as my yard matured into the desired wildlife habitat that I'd hoped for, and began producing its own seeds and fruits and insects for the birds, I stopped buying bird feed and solved the squirrel problem.

Not too long afterward, though, I began to notice that elongated patches of bark were missing from the smaller branches of some of my trees. Upon close inspection, I could see little incisor marks, like miniatures of those that beavers make. Hmm! Indeed, it was the squirrels that were feeding on the nutritious cambium layer of the branches. Like beavers, squirrels are rodents and when nuts and seeds are less plentiful—or perhaps just to vary their diet—the squirrels know that they can always get a decent meal of cambium. Unfortunately, if there is an overabundance of squirrels, they can wreak relative havoc with both ornamental and native trees.

My arborist friends here in the upper Willamette Valley confirm my observations and note that squirrels seem to eat the cambium of conifers as readily as that of broad-leafed trees. If squirrels remove the bark from just one side of the branch, the wound will eventually close over or "heal." But if the branch is completely girdled, it will die. I've seen both Oregon white oaks and northern red oaks in our area where a significant portion of the tree canopy is dead as a result of squirrels.

Locally, there are three species of diurnal (active during the day) tree squirrels. In urban and suburban areas, the *eastern fox squirrel* prevails. It is native to forests east of the Great Plains, but was introduced here many years ago. It appears to be more adaptable and aggressive than the native *western gray squirrel*, which increases in abundance only as one nears the edges of metro areas. The two are easy to tell apart, as the non-native fox squirrel has reddish-brown fur and a pale yellow to orange belly while gray squirrels are silver-gray above with a white belly and a bushier tail. A third species called the *chickaree* (or Douglas squirrel) is usually found in rural coniferous forests. It's smaller than the other two and has dark reddish-olive fur (a bit grayer in winter) and a yellowish belly.

In addition to the damage they sometimes inflict on trees, western gray and eastern fox squirrels can be nuisances in filbert and walnut orchards. If control measures are necessary, orchardists need to know that fox squirrels can be removed any time during the year because they are an exotic (non-native) species. The native grays, on the other hand, are protected in Oregon as a game animal and can be hunted only in season (usually September and October) or with a special permit.

Because squirrels in built-up areas really have few predators other than automobiles, their numbers are limited mostly by the availability of food. So in neighborhoods where nut-bearing trees, unprotected birdfeeders, and people who put out peanuts are abundant, squirrels are likely to proliferate. The most sensible way, then, to keep squirrel populations at a moderate level is to watch those birdfeeders and keep those peanuts to yourself.

Remember, too, that any attempt to limit squirrel numbers by live-trapping or other means is mostly an exercise in futility, as new squirrels from outside the area will quickly move in to fill the vacuum. In an effort to keep squirrels away from his birdfeeders, my father one year live-trapped fifty of them and released them several miles away in a wooded area. And at the end of the year, there were just as many squirrels at the feeders as before.

(This article first appeared in the 28 October 1998 edition of
The Springfield News.)

PORT-ORFORD-CEDAR

THIS ATTRACTIVE CONIFER was once commonly planted in our area. It is most easily distinguished from the three other "cedar-like" conifers native to Oregon and planted in gardens—all of which produce fern-like sprays of flattened needles—by its cones which are spherical and pea-sized. But unlike the other three species—western red-cedar, Alaska yellow-cedar, and incense-cedar—Port-Orford-cedar is highly susceptible to a root disease that is fatal to the trees.

You might have noticed local conifers that suddenly turn reddish-brown, with not a green needle left on the whole tree. These are Port-Orford-cedars (*Chamaecyparis lawsoniana*) that have contracted Port-Orford-cedar root disease. The disease is caused by a fungus that lives in the soil and kills *only* Port-Orford-cedars. The infection begins via the tree's root system and kills the tissues near the base of the tree, preventing the tree from transporting water and nutrients to its canopy. So the tree dies.

Although Port-Orford-cedar, as its name implies, is native to southwestern Oregon—as well as northwestern California—the fungus that is killing these trees both in the wild and in cultivation apparently arrived from Asia in the early 1900s. It quickly killed the trees growing in nurseries and, in the following decades, has continued to spread in parks and gardens throughout the maritime Northwest, as well as in the forests where Port-Orford-cedar is native.

In the wild, logging trucks and recreational vehicles are the most common ways that the spores of the disease are moved over any distance, but elk hooves, hikers' boots, and other means can also spread the disease locally. Spores can infect entire watersheds, too, by moving underground in wet soil, or in streams. In cultivated areas, the root disease is spread by lawnmower tires, muddy boots, or even birds and other animals which can carry a small amount of infected soil on their feet. In short, there's not much we can do to prevent its continued spread.

What is especially tragic is that Port-Orford-cedar was for many years a popular hedge plant. These hedges, long since overgrown, have turned into long lines of attractive, graceful trees. When one tree in the line becomes infected with the disease and dies, the rest of the trees quickly succumb as the fungus spreads rapidly underground from one tree to the next.

Ten-year-old Port-Orford-cedar.

It is unlikely that the disease will ever find and kill all of our area's Port-Orford-cedars—just as Dutch elm disease has not found and killed every elm. So I encourage the replanting of these lovely trees—one here and two or three there, instead of in long rows of the same species. They grow relatively fast, are adapted to our winter-wet and summer-dry climate, and deserve a place in our gardens and parks.

Because Port-Orford-cedars are no longer grown by nurseries, there is an obvious problem of availability. But seedlings can often be found in the vicinity of established trees, and new trees can also be started by rooting cuttings.

And, thanks to the work done over the past decade or so by the USDA Forest Service Dorena Genetic Resource Center—located just east of Cottage Grove—we may someday once again be able to find these lovely trees in nurseries. Within the Port-Orford-cedar species, some natural resistance to this non-native disease occurs. By purposely infecting thousands of seedlings, then crossing the survivors, infecting their progeny again, and so on, researchers have been able to produce a small number of individual trees that appear to be almost completely resistant to Port-Orford-cedar root disease. Seedlings of these trees may eventually be made available to reforestation agencies—for planting in the wild to restore Port-Orford-cedar's place in the forests from which it has been lost—as well as to the public, for planting as cultivated trees in parks and gardens.

One of the oldest surviving Port-Orford-cedars in Eugene stands at the northwest corner of Collier House on the University of Oregon campus. This tree appears in a photograph taken about 1900—when the tree was about five years old—and is still in good health. Although this individual may escape the root disease for another year or even another century, it is highly likely that, eventually, it will succumb.

To ensure that Port-Orford-cedars continue to grace the landscapes of western Oregon campuses, parks, and gardens, we need to consider implementing a planting program that will introduce, as soon as possible, disease-resistant individuals so that, a hundred years from now, Eugeneans will still be able to admire one of the loveliest of Oregon's many native conifers.

Close-up of ripening seed cones on Port-Orford-cedar.

(This article first appeared in the Winter 2011 edition of *ETF News*.)

GREENS CAN LAST UNTIL EARLY SPRING

ONE OF MY FAVORITE EARLY-WINTER ACTIVITIES as a child was going into the woods with my family to gather greens. Because I lived then in the middle of the great eastern hardwood forest in Pennsylvania, there weren't a lot of greens to be found, as most of the plants were deciduous. But we'd collect white pine boughs and running-pine, a kind of vining forest groundcover that grew in certain special places in the woods.

After our little treasure hunt, we'd head home and make wreaths and swags for the doors and windows, both inside and outside the house. And we'd place greens atop the piano and hang them from the mantle over the fireplace. Everything smelled so good and it somehow made the cold winter days feel just a little warmer.

Here in western Oregon, the use of seasonal greens around the house can also be helpful in boosting morale at this time of year when the days are so short and often so dark and gray. Unlike Pennsylvanians, we Oregonians are truly blessed with an enormous variety of plants, both native and non-native, from which to choose our greenery. And because of our humid winter climate, those greens can last until early spring outside.

Inside, depending on how warm and dry our houses are, they can still last at least a few weeks. Of course, dried greens can always be replaced with fresh ones throughout the winter, too.

The obvious choices for greens in this area include native conifers such as Douglas-fir and noble fir. Douglas-fir, as every Oregonian knows, is ubiquitous at lower elevations. To find noble fir, you'll often need to walk through some snow, as these trees grow mostly above 4,000 feet elevation in the Cascades. There are also grand fir at lower elevations and sub-alpine fir up near the mountain passes. All of these greens are wonderfully fragrant.

Then there are the cedars such as western redcedar, Port-Orford-cedar (which grows wild along the south coast), and incense-cedar. The boughs of all these trees lend themselves especially well to garlands and swags. Other regionally native conifers include Sitka spruce and western hemlock, but neither of these conifers retains its needles very well after being cut. In addition to the many native conifers, there are all kinds of cultivated conifers whose greens can be used, from coast redwoods and giant sequoias to Colorado spruces and Himalayan cedars.

Trees aren't the only source of greens. Many broad-leafed evergreen shrubs, both native and non-native, also make beautiful wintertime decorations. The native salal (suh-LAL) has broad, leathery, shiny green leaves that contrast nicely with the more finely textured conifers. Salal is a common understory shrub in area forests and is used to a very limited extent as a landscape plant. Oregon-grape and swordfern are other beautiful additions to arrangements, both indoors and out. Add to that the lovely foliage of cultivated shrubs such as camellia and photinia, and the selection is almost endless.

One of my favorite ways to use greens is in outdoor planters—window boxes, tubs, and the like—that would otherwise sit empty all winter. I just take 12- to 18-inch-long pieces of salal, Oregon-grape, and Douglas-fir (the stiffer boughs of young firs work better than the more droopy boughs of older trees) and insert them into the potting soil, making sure to use plenty of greens to make a nice, dense mass. Provided the containers remain out in the open where they'll be rained on, these greens will look nice all winter long.

You might also consider making small gifts of greens for friends and neighbors, especially those who cannot get outside much in winter. Just fill a six-inch clay pot with damp peat, then poke the desired greens into the peat, add a ribbon, and you've made an attractive, inexpensive decoration for someone special.

If you're using greens indoors, one way to make them last longer is to keep them moist. That can be accomplished by making "arrangements" in damp peat (as mentioned above) and then being sure to keep an eye on the peat so it doesn't dry out. Or you can just make bouquets of greens in a vase filled with water, just as we do for flowers. Some of the cultivated greens work especially well in this way. For example, Japanese aucuba (uh-KOO-buh)—a fairly common shrub in shady gardens—can last for weeks in a vase of water on your coffee table.

Again, there's no need to limit one's use of greens to the holiday season. Because they are so abundant in our area and can last such a long time, depending on how and where they are used, you can be surrounded by cut greens from early November until early April.

And once these cheery additions to our homes and gardens begin to wither, just place them outside beneath your shrubs, or snip them up into your compost, and let nature recycle all their nutrients and organic matter into more greens to brighten your winter days another year.

(This article first appeared in the 22 December 1999 edition of *The Springfield News*.)

NEVER A BORING AUTUMN

I T'S THAT SEASON AGAIN when much of the arborescent greenery of summer turns orange or purple or gold or brown (remember, brown is a color, too) just before dropping. Fall color already begins in our area in late September and continues until well after Thanksgiving most years, thanks to our mild, ocean-influenced climate that greatly extends our springs and falls.

White Ash
(*Fraxinus americana*)

The first trees to change color and then lose their leaves are the katsuras (*Cercidiphyllum japonicum*) from Japan, followed closely by the ashes. By the time you receive this newsletter, most of the ashes may already be leafless, but fall will still be just starting! There are maples and lindens and oaks and many other kinds of trees whose leaves will be changing color in the last half of October or later, so if you were out of town the first half, you'll still have plenty of color to enjoy.

Phenology is the study of how periodic biological phenomena such as flowering, peak fall color, and leaf drop are related to weather. Just as different species of trees and other plants always bloom in the same order every year—but slightly earlier or later in the season due to variable weather conditions from one year to the next—the native as well as non-native deciduous trees whose leaves turn color here in fall always do so in the same order. That's why I can tell you without looking out the window that it's Ash Time now, as I write this, and that Oak Time will come later. It always does. While it's true that predictability can in some cases lead to boredom, I've never yet experienced a boring autumn!

(This article first appeared in the Fall 2007 edition of *ETF News*.)

SENTRY-LIKE COAST REDWOOD
SURVIVES DEVASTATING STORM

ON THE AFTERNOON OF THE RECENT WINDSTORM, I had the misfortune to be sitting inside a bus, returning to the Springfield-Eugene area from my day in the woods up near McKenzie Bridge. I could tell from the wildly waving Douglas-firs along the highway that this was no ordinary storm, and I wanted to be out in it. But there I was, trapped between panes of tinted glass and hurtling along at 55 miles per hour.

I thought of John Muir's story about the stormy night he spent clinging to the top of a tall conifer somewhere in the California Sierra, as the wind tossed the tree and him around and back and forth, much to his delight. It's not that I wanted to be riding out the storm high in a conifer myself; it's just that I didn't want to be riding it out in a bus.

All I wanted was to be outside and to feel the wind in my face and smell the air fragrant with the scent of fir needles from the thousands of broken branchlets that were flying through the air all around us. But no. There wasn't a breath of air in the bus, and not even the faintest whiff of Douglas-fir.

Fortunately, I had in my pocket some sprigs of western redcedar and grand fir that I had picked just before leaving the woods an hour earlier. So I took them out and rubbed them gently to release their wonderful aroma. To be sure, it wasn't the same as being outside, but it helped me to tolerate my temporary confinement.

Once we were back in town, my excitement over the storm changed to apprehension as the bus I transferred to was detoured once, then twice, to avoid downed trees that were blocking city streets. My redwood tree! What's happened to my redwood tree? (I live downwind from an enormous, lovely, two-trunked coast redwood that rises like a green exclamation point in a neighborhood of mostly small houses and small trees.)

As I approached my street, I craned my neck to see if I could catch sight of the top of the redwood. Would it be okay? Would it still be standing, sentry-like, guarding my house and those of my neighbors? Indeed, as I rounded the last corner, I could see my beloved pillar of green still standing tall. Oh, it had that tousled look that is always gets after a storm moves through, but it was still standing. Lucky tree, lucky me.

Elsewhere in our community, of course, the scene was different. Many hundreds of trees were toppled, and thousands lost significant parts of their canopies. Most of the fallen or damaged trees were older, larger individuals. Some of them, like the huge bigleaf maple in the 1200 block of Mill Street in Eugene, I will greatly miss. For most of my adult life, I've passed beneath them regularly, never failing to be awed by their magnificence.

At the same time that I mourn the loss of so many trees, I cannot help but be amazed that the vast majority of our community's trees are still standing. Although many of the fallen trees had significant amounts of rot in their trunks or roots, some of them were completely sound. By the same token, many of the trees left standing probably have a lot of rot in them. Why didn't they fall?

These days, most of us are adherents of rationalism, the idea that everything that happens in this world has a reason and can be explained. Our sciences, our legal system, and our society as a whole are based on rationalism. How do plants grow? We can figure that out. Why did my car run into that other car? We can find out what to blame or to whom to point the finger.

But I am persuaded that some events cannot be explained. The only reason that some trees blew down is that they were in the wrong place at the wrong time, as we say. And the only reason that some are still standing is that they were lucky. This kind of thinking, of course, flies in the face of everything I have been taught. And that's okay. Because, little by little, as I've grown older, I've realized that some of the things my most revered professors and teachers taught me were not (gasp!) in fact true.

The simple fact that "my" redwood is still standing, unscarred by the storm, while a virtually identical redwood at the nearby University of Oregon campus lost its top and many of its branches, can in my mind be ascribed to nothing more than luck. It's not necessarily because one of the trees is stronger or has better genes than the other.

So give your favorite old tree a friendly pat now and then. The reason that it's still standing might well be that it has good genes or that it has been properly pruned. But remember, too, that one reason that it's still standing might just be that it's a lucky tree. And by patting it, some of its luck might rub off on you.

(This article first appeared in the 2 March 2002 edition of
The Springfield News.)

TREES AND THE "LATE" SNOW

WHEN EUGENEANS AWOKE on the first full day of spring this year, they looked out upon a decidedly un-springlike landscape, with snow covering everything and still falling at a steady rate. By the time it stopped mid-morning, there were some seven inches on the ground on the valley floor.

Although the scene looked like a Christmas card, it definitely did not sound like one. No sleigh bells ringing in the distance, or carolers rounding the corner and breaking into yet another seasonal favorite. Instead, many parts of Eugene echoed with what sounded eerily like gunshots, as branches—and in some cases entire trees—snapped under the weight of the unusually wet and heavy snow.

The streets in some neighborhoods were barely passable, as still-laden tree branches arched over toward the center of the street, and already fallen branches lay silently on the asphalt, while their brethren continued to groan under the snow's weight, uncertain of whether they could bear the load or, like their already fallen comrades, have to yield to it by breaking.

The snow took an especially heavy toll on early-spring blooming trees such as flowering plums, saucer magnolias, and Callery pears. Because these trees had already budded out, there was more surface area for the wet snow to cling to, so less snow was able to sift through the trees' canopies to end up on the ground.

Other trees that took it hard included English hawthorns and lacebark elms, both of which have relatively dense, twiggy canopies. Even though these trees hadn't yet begun to break bud, they still held a lot more snow than many other species, and breakage was common.

Of course, some traditionally storm-strong tree species such as London plane trees fared very well overall. But even those trees underwent "natural pruning" by having already-dead twigs and branches brought down to the ground by the snow.

Although evergreen conifers are generally thought of as being resilient during heavy snowfalls—since many species are native to higher elevations or parts of the world with consistently snowy winters—some of the local, low-elevation conifers such as Douglas-fir suffered quite a bit. The firs have relatively dense canopies that, as mentioned above, hold more snow than trees with more open canopies. In addition, when branches in the trees' upper canopies (which hold the *most* snow) break, they fall onto the branches just beneath them and, with increasing momentum, hurtle earthward, taking with them one branch after the other.

The post-storm carnage on the east side of the 2700 block of Harris Street.

Native Oregon white oaks and Oregon ashes suffered considerably, too, as their wet-season lichen and moss loads were at peak development, so just like the early-flowering trees, their branches held more wet snow than tree canopies with less abundant lichens and mosses.

City public works staff—and neighbors, too—did an admirable job cleaning up most of the debris in a surprisingly short time. Much work remains to be done in our parks and open spaces, which are rightly not prioritized after a storm like this. In wilder parks such as Spencer Butte, most of the debris will simply be left on the ground to decompose and to provide a host of important ecological benefits as it does so. Trails, of course, will be cleared and made accessible once again.

Did the storm "teach" us anything about urban tree selection and care? Not really. We've had storms of this and greater magnitude in the past. (In January 1969, more than 47 inches of snow fell on Eugene!) As usual, the faster-growing, softer-wooded trees such as flowering plums and cottonwoods took it the hardest. And the branches and trunks of other species with extensive rot or other structural problems just ended up on the ground a bit sooner than they otherwise might have.

For our street-side trees growing in the public right-of-way, a priority now is to evaluate the severely damaged trees and determine which ones can truly be salvaged—that is, can they resume healthy, solid growth? Those that cannot need to be removed as soon as possible, the stumps ground, and new trees planted. That's how nature works after a "disturbance"—windstorm, fire, disease—and that's exactly what our community should emulate following a storm like The Big Snow of March 2012.

(This article first appeared in the Spring 2012 newsletter of *Friends of Trees.*)

IT'S TULIP-TREE TIME

THE TULIP-TREE IS COMMON in the deciduous hardwood forests of eastern North America, where it can soar to heights in excess of 100 feet on some sites. Its most distinctive features are its unique leaves—which have four to six lobes—and its beautiful, tulip-like flowers which appear in spring after the leaves are already developed. The botanical name for tulip-tree is itself beautiful: *Liriodendron tulipifera* means "tulip-bearing lily tree." Ahh!

Close-up of tulip-tree flower in late spring.

Here in Eugene, the tulip-tree is neither common nor particularly rare. But perhaps because it is not generally available in local nurseries, few of them are planted. It is a fast-growing tree that is closely related to the magnolias. In fact, the pink-petaled magnolia that in local gardens blooms before it leafs out in spring—which most of us elsewhere in the United States call a saucer magnolia (*Magnolia × soulangeana*)—is referred to in California as a "tulip-tree," too.

One place to see tulip-trees in central Eugene is on the west side of the Lane County Elections building—at the northeast corner of 10th and Lincoln—because the branches of those trees are low enough to permit passersby to admire the flowers, which appear in May. And at 1176 Polk Street, there is a pair of large trees growing in the park strip.

Tulip-trees grow best around here on deep river loam soils and on irrigated soils away from the valley floor. They do not do well on the poorly drained soils of our "clay neighborhoods," where ashes, sweetgums, pin oaks and other trees native to swamps are better choices.

One drawback of the tulip-tree in our area is its susceptibility to aphids (perhaps due to our dry and relatively dirty summer air, compared to the humid and rainy summers where it is native) which drip their sticky "exudate" onto pavements, vehicles, and people beneath the tree's canopy. Nevertheless, it is a magnificent tree whose flowers are a sight to see at this time of year.

(This article first appeared in the Spring 2007 edition of *ETF News*.)

TREES ARE THE NATURAL LANDSCAPE
IN WESTERN OREGON

WHEN I BOUGHT MY HOUSE some five years ago, the lot was dominated by grass. At one time, it had evidently been a lawn that was mowed regularly. But it hadn't been mowed in many months, and by the time I moved in, in late June, the lawn had become a real meadow. It was certainly attractive, both aesthetically, to the human eye and mind, and ecologically—to myriad beneficial insects, birds, and other organisms that appreciated the cover provided by the tall grasses and clovers, and the seeds they produced.

I spent the remainder of the summer trying to decide how best to care for this little piece of property of which I was now the steward. My options were several. I could cut the meadow and begin mowing again on a regular basis. After all, I already had a mower; I knew how to mow; and of course, that's what all of my neighbors do.

My second option was to take a lesson from the lot's previous steward—or *non*-steward, if his meadow was in fact the result of laziness rather than a purposeful decision—and leave it in meadow. I'd cut it once a year, in early summer. Not a bad idea. It would be very little work for me, while at the same time providing important habitat for wildlife.

Third, I thought I could call upon my training in horticulture and landscape design and create a so-called display garden, with interesting flowers and shrubs from all over the world. It would certainly be pretty to look at. But it would take constant attention to keep it looking its best, plus I'd have to irrigate in summer and occasionally fight off insect pests or diseases that pampered, non-native plants are sometimes prone to. I do enjoy hard work, but I'd rather not engage in an ongoing battle against pests and weeds and the like, just to have my tidy little "zoo" of unusual plants.

My fourth option was to follow Nature's example and let the site become woodland—or at least the part of it that wasn't needed to grow fruits and vegetables. Virtually every square foot of land west of the Cascades crest wants to become forested. Only rocky bluffs, open water, and moving sand dunes are truly safe from the encroaching forest. Granted, the upper Willamette Valley was largely treeless when Euro-American settlers arrived here in the mid-1800s, but that's only because the series of cultures that had inhabited the valley before them set fire to the valley floor on a regular enough basis to *keep* trees from growing here.

Each of the four options had its attributes. But only the fourth option would create for me a largely maintenance-free landscape. So my choice was easy. I would of course have plenty of other opportunities for physical exercise and for use of my horticultural skills by producing food for the household. The rest of the site would largely care for itself.

That fall, *afforestation* of the site commenced—that is, the planting of trees on a site that was treeless before. I selected native tree species that were suited to the site's soil and began planting. For the first few years, a young woodland needs periodic attention to encourage the new trees and discourage interlopers such as blackberry and grasses. But eventually, the trees start doing what comes naturally and grow both up and out, shading more of the ground with every year that passes and doing a great job at eliminating weeds, most of which are sun-loving.

Over time, then, the seeds of native shrubs and wildflowers are introduced by birds or, in my case, I introduced them myself because there were so few natural sources nearby. And I am not at all embarrassed to say that I spend precious little time—or little precious time—maintaining the developing woodland.

In the coming decades, I can selectively remove trees and sell the wood for lumber or for firewood, and then replant. Or some future owner might choose to let the trees grow to maturity, then outright "log" the site and replant. It makes sense to me to grow some of our timber right here in town, where most of us live, instead of trucking it in from the nearby hills and beyond.

A quick glance around the Springfield-Eugene metropolitan area reveals many large sites well suited to afforestation. Most of them are in the public right-of-way along major highways. Currently, these areas are dominated by grasses that require a substantial amount of manpower, machinery, and money to maintain. Other areas are covered with English ivy, recently declared a "noxious" plant by Oregon's Department of Agriculture.

Imagine visitors to our area arriving via Interstate 5 fifty years from now and driving through an attractive, forested corridor. "What foresight," they'll say, "that the people who lived here back at the beginning of the century thought to thread their highway carefully through this lovely forest, instead of cutting it down and planting grass and other plants that required constant care and provided very few ecological benefits."

They won't realize, of course, that the forest through which they are driving was not preserved during highway construction, but was planted well after the highway was completed. No matter. Landscapes change, and so do our perceptions of them.

Highway planners and engineers will quickly come up with a list of reasons why we should *not* restore woodlands and forests along our highways:

- Reason No. 1: "Safety hazard." (Someone might veer off the road and run into a tree.) So why don't we cut down all the trees that currently grow along all of our state highways that pass through heavily forested areas?
- Reason No. 2: "Fire hazard." (Trees are flammable.) How many forest fires are started every year along Highway 126 to the coast? *Grass* fires, on the other hand, are relatively common (to wit, the large blackened areas at the I-5/I-105 interchange this past summer).
- Reason No. 3: "High maintenance costs." (Trees and shrubs planted along highways require pruning and other care.) But nobody spends a cent to maintain the forested corridors through the Cascades and along the southern end of I-205 near Portland.

Any more reasons not to do this, guys? So let's get planting. We hire a reforestation crew and have them treat our bleak roadsides as recent clearcuts. That is, have them plant the areas with Douglas-firs and other suitable native conifers, with a few broad-leafed trees such as bigleaf maple and Oregon ash, where appropriate. Keep an eye on things the first few years, until the trees start to take off, then provide periodic, light-handed care as the woodland develops. Bingo! We're home free.

I recall reading the comment of a Greyhound bus passenger after the bus driver suffered a fatal heart attack at the wheel and the bus careened out of control above a 400-foot drop-off along Coast Highway 101 near Otter Rock (*The Register-Guard*, 9 December 1998). The bus broke through a guard rail and came to rest against the trees growing on the steep hillside, and the passengers escaped into the predawn darkness with nothing more than scratches.

"If it wasn't for those trees, we would have been tossed salad," she remarked. "I say, plant 100,000 trees along the freeways for safety."

I rest my case.

(This article first appeared in the 5 October 2002 edition of *The Springfield News.*)

SOIL VOLUME, TREE CANOPY, AND THE IMPORTANCE OF BEING VIGILANT

IN EUGENE'S EARLY DAYS, you could plant almost any kind of tree anywhere and it would be assured of a relatively long and healthy life—as long as a "parked" horse didn't chew off the tree's bark. Eugene was founded, after all, by farmers who knew good soil when they saw it. The fertile, deep, and well-drained loam of the Willamette River's floodplain was ideal for growing food crops as well as trees that would shade the first streets of Eugene City.

But over the years, the wonderful loam that underlies downtown has been displaced by basements, utility trenches, gravel, rubble, and everything else that ends up underground in a modern city. As a result, the good soil that at one time seemed limitless in its extent has become increasingly scarce. And the trees that we plant downtown end up living shorter and more disease-prone lives as their roots seek—but are unable to find—the soil that trees need to develop large, healthy canopies.

Because available soil volume is now the major constraint limiting tree growth in our downtown, Eugene Tree Foundation often speaks up on behalf of soil protection and preservation, to help ensure the health and longevity of new trees planted downtown.

The best time to speak up is early in the planning process, when developers and architects are just beginning to make decisions about building placement, construction techniques, and so forth. For most of these professionals, soil is just "dirt" which does not have value until something is built upon it. Many of these same people, however, appreciate our plant friends and include trees and other vegetation in their plans, but their drawings usually show just the plants' above-ground parts, ignoring the plants' underground needs.

A case in point is a condominium project called The Tate which is nearing completion at 1375 Olive Street. Before construction began, permission was granted to remove a half-dozen healthy, 20-year-old white ash trees growing in the publicly owned park strip in front of the development site (to allow easier access for the construction contractor) with the stipulation that the trees be replaced with new trees upon completion of the project. A letter from Eugene Tree Foundation emphasizing the need to protect large volumes of soil during downtown projects—or else import the soil following project completion and before planting trees—was sent to Eugene's mayor and city councilors, referring in particular to circumstances at The Tate.

After the completion of the building, as the landscape contractor was beginning his work (which was to include the planting of the new street trees), an alert passerby noticed that instead of replacing the compacted soil in the park strip with good soil, it was replaced with crushed rock, which does not grow trees. Moreover, the passerby learned that instead of large-canopy trees being planted to replace the broad-spreading white ashes, a columnar maple cultivar was to be planted, at the request of the property owners (who evidently wanted to limit the leaf fall onto the one-story portion of their building).

The project's owners were immediately contacted, as well as the city's urban forestry staff and the project's landscape architect, and a discussion followed. Most of the rock ended up being removed and replaced with loam, and the columnar maple cultivar was replaced with a green ash cultivar called 'Summit' that will eventually form a broader-canopied tree as it matures.

Newly planted trees at The Tate on Olive Street in downtown Eugene.

As is often the case, the site owners, city staff, and the landscape architect all apparently had the best of intentions before and during construction, but there were still problems. And because landscaping is usually the last task to accomplish before the deadline for project completion and final inspections, corners are sometimes cut that might otherwise not be cut. And the trees end up taking it in the roots, so to speak.

The moral of this story? Speak up on behalf of trees! They cannot do it themselves; they depend on us. Sometimes, despite the best efforts of city staff, project architects, and property owners, trees still lose out. Eugene's small urban forestry staff, in particular, cannot keep tabs on every single development site.

So if you see something regarding trees that just looks wrong to you, speak first to the project manager or site owner about your concern by raising questions, rather than telling them what you think they should be doing. If their answers fail to satisfy you, call the city urban forestry staff (682-4800) who depend on the eyes of the rest of us out in the community to see the violations or shortcomings they cannot see. They are very good at following up citizens' tips.

Here are a few tips on being a more effective Dendro-Vigilante (!):

- Intercede early and often on behalf of trees (project managers and site owners appreciate knowing as early as possible about these concerns)

- Be pleasant and respectful of those with whom you talk (if you're really upset by what you see, try to settle down before pursuing things)

- Follow up your "victories" as well as your "defeats" with a thank-you-for-your-consideration card (you will likely be remembered in a favorable light, regardless of the outcome)

You don't have to be an arborist, a landscape architect, or a community activist to speak up on behalf of trees. All you need to be is someone interested in the welfare of our community's trees. And that's a perfect description of *you*, isn't it?

(This article first appeared in the Summer 2006 edition of *ETF News*.)

THE WIND IN THE TREES

MANY PEOPLE ARE AWARE of the apparent effect of strong winds on trees that grow along the coast and on exposed ridges in the high mountains. The trunks of trees in these locations that sometimes experience severe weather may be strongly slanted or bent, and the crowns or canopies of the trees are often very asymmetrical. But few people realize that, even where relatively gentle weather prevails most of the time, such as here in the upper Willamette Valley, wind can cause significant *crown deformation* in both native and cultivated trees.

Interestingly, trees at the coast and in the mountains are not deformed due to the wind, per se. At the coast, for example, the strongest winds occur in the wintertime as storms arrive from the Pacific Ocean, generally from the *southwest*. But tree canopies there are deformed as if a wind from the *northwest* were acting on them! How can that be? Well, what causes the deformation of coastal tree canopies is not the wind itself, but the salt that is carried on the wind—which kills the tissues, buds, and leaves or needles on the windward side of the tree.

During the winter, storms off the ocean are accompanied by rain, which washes any salt off. But during the summer, the strong north-northwest winds that blow almost daily along Oregon's coast deposit salt on the *northwest* sides of trees that does *not* wash off, resulting in the *southeast* side of the tree (out of reach of the salt) growing more luxuriantly than the northwest side and thus over time creating the lopsided canopy.

In the mountains, the effects on trees are similar. There, however, it is a wintertime phenomenon and what causes the crown deformation is not salt, but blowing snow, ice, and abrasive volcanic materials, all of which kill tissues, buds, and needles on the windward side of the tree and create an asymmetrical canopy.

Okay, back to the Willamette Valley. Here in the Eugene-Springfield area, part of what makes our summers so exceedingly pleasant—compared with many other parts of the state and country—is that, even when it's occasionally very hot, we almost always benefit from a strong diurnal wind that develops by mid-morning on most days and lasts until about sunset.

Because this is a growing-season wind, and it occurs over a period of many weeks, it affects the canopy development of many (but not all) species of trees growing here. Broad-leafed trees tend to be more affected than conifers, for example, and some species of broad-leafed trees much more than others.

Some members of the magnolia family (magnolias and tulip-trees) are particularly vulnerable to crown deformation. So are London plane-trees (*Platanus x acerifolia*) and some species of ash (*Fraxinus*). The pink-flowered and frequently planted 'Kwanzan' cultivar of Japanese flowering cherry (*Prunus serrulata*) is also very susceptible.

The two oak species native to this area—Oregon white oak (*Quercus garryana*) and California black oak (*Quercus kelloggii*)—respond very differently. The former is never deformed by these strong daytime winds; the latter almost always is, exhibiting both a leaning trunk and deformed crown.

Perhaps understandably, the most deformed trees are found in the most exposed locations where the daily winds are strongest. Such trees can be at the north edge of town—adjacent to open fields, across which the wind can really rip—or in downtown "canyons" or in parks with extensive open areas (e.g., Amazon Park), or in large parking lots. Conversely, the crowns of trees growing in courtyards or in heavily treed neighborhoods tend to be relatively unaffected by the wind.

The direction in which affected trees lean can tell us a lot about wind patterns in and around the Eugene-Springfield area. In Eugene, the diurnal summer winds are out of the north, and affected trees lean due south. But as one heads east in the metropolitan area toward the Cascades, prevailing wind direction shifts by 90 degrees!

This is especially evident as one drives eastbound from Eugene along the I-105 freeway and Highway 126. West of the I-5 interchange, while still in Eugene, all affected trees point to the south. But soon after crossing I-5 to Springfield, tree canopies begin tilting a little bit to the east of south, then toward the southeast, then east-southeast, and finally due east—all in a matter of just a few miles! Why is this? Two reasons: 1) here in the upper Willamette Valley the north wind is confined to the valley by the Coburg Hills on the east side of the valley, and as soon as the wind gets past the Coburgs, it is able to fan out toward the east; and 2) the McKenzie Valley has its own up-valley diurnal wind that is "sucking" air out of the Willamette Valley west of it.

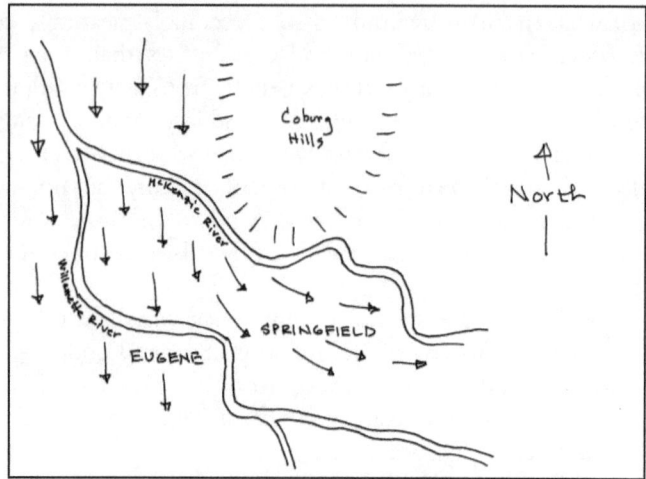

*Prevailing direction of diurnal summer winds in the Eugene-Springfield area,
as indicated by crown deformation in "wind-deformed" tree species.*

Another effect of these strong, hot, dry winds can be seen in local dawn redwoods (*Metasequoia glyptostroboïdes*). These deciduous conifers— "discovered" only in the 1940s in a remote area of south-central China— are native to an area where summers are warm and humid. In similar climates outside of that area—such as in Washington, DC and elsewhere east of the Great Plains—the trees (most of them less than 60 years of age) have grown very fast and maintained a strong central leader, as most conifers do. Here in Eugene, however, the vertical growth of dawn redwoods is relatively slow in exposed areas. Or, if the tree develops well during its early years in the lee of other trees or buildings, then gets *above* those trees or buildings, its upward growth is quickly curtailed.

A good example of this effect is the dawn redwood on the University of Oregon campus (just southwest of the Science Library) that is one of the oldest in North America—but shorter than some trees elsewhere in the United States that are half its age. The top growth of this individual has all but halted, now that the tree's tip has grown past the protection afforded by the buildings to its north.

So keep your eyes open as you explore the Eugene-Springfield area, and look for the effect of wind on the trees. Again, not all species are affected by our strong summer winds, and trees growing in the most exposed areas show more dramatic effects than those of the same species that grow in more protected areas. Finally, remember that the "bad" wind that is strong and frequent enough to deform the crowns of some local trees is at the same time the "good" wind that makes warm and sometimes hot summer days here especially pleasant for human beings.

(This article first appeared in the Summer 2012 newsletter of
Friends of Trees.)

TREES PLAN AHEAD

WINTERTIME IS THE DORMANT SEASON for trees here in the Willamette Valley. But as daylength and average daily temperature increase over the next few weeks, alarm clocks will begin ringing in the arboreal world and the trees will commence another season of growth.

One intriguing aspect of tree physiology is how far ahead trees "plan" for the following year's growth. Most broad-leafed trees (e.g., maples, oaks, ashes) and conifers already began to develop their 2007–8 winter buds last spring, and completed bud formation by the end of June or, at the latest, early July 2007.

Inside those buds is a miniaturized version of *every* organ—twig, leaf, flower—that will develop in spring 2008 after bud "break" occurs and the bud scales that protected the bud all winter fall away and the new shoot starts to elongate. In trees with exceptionally large buds such as horse-chestnuts (*Aesculus* species), it's easy to dissect the bud and see what is waiting in the wings inside. Simply slice the bud lengthwise and take a peek. For an even better look, dissect the halved bud with a needle or tweezers and you'll be able to unfold and examine the individual organs. Amazing!

From left: a tightly closed horsechestnut bud; a dissected bud showing all the immature organs inside; and the characteristic hand-like palmate leaf of the horsechestnut (after being carefully removed from the intact bud).

(This article first appeared in the Winter 2008 edition of *ETF News*.)

GOLDENCHAIN TREE

ARELATIVELY LITTLE-KNOWN, spring-flowering tree that grows perfectly well in the Eugene area is the goldenchain tree (*Laburnum x watereri*). As the "x" in its botanical name indicates, it is a horticultural hybrid of two other laburnum species—*Laburnum alpinum* and *Laburnum anagyroïdes*—so it exists only in cultivation and not in the wild. The parents of this hybrid are both native to Europe, and are themselves attractive plants, but they are planted even less often than the hybrid.

It is a small tree of upright habit and oval form that is showiest in mid-spring when the canopy is festooned with long, pendulous clusters of bright yellow, pea-like flowers set against a backdrop of the tree's fresh green foliage. The flower clusters very much resemble—except in color—those of wisteria, to which it is related (they're both in the pea family or Fabaceae).

Although the British refer to all species of the genus *Laburnum* as "laburnums," American horticulturists call the trees "goldenchain trees." This can create some confusion because there is another tree that blooms here in the upper (or southern) Willamette Valley later in the season—typically the first half of July—that is called the golden*rain* tree (*Koelreuteria paniculata*). The latter has very large clusters of tiny yellow flowers that resemble a "golden rain" as they fall from the tree—and afterward lie on the ground beneath the tree. (For best results, you need a little imagination.)

Goldenchain trees have compound leaves comprised of three leaflets. The trees grow best if provided with well-drained soil and plenty of sun. They bloom every year, but some years—referred to as "good laburnum years" in Britain—they seem to truly outdo themselves.

Close-up of the pendulous clusters of goldenchain tree flowers in spring.

(This article first appeared in the Spring 2010 edition of *ETF News.*)

SUMMER DROUGHT CAUSES LEAF DROP

SOME DECIDUOUS TREES on unirrigated sites naturally lose a portion of their leaves as our annual summer drought here in the upper Willamette Valley intensifies in late summer. It's their way of economizing on the limited soil water available at that time of year. That's because broad, lush leaves are relatively big water wasters in a winter-wet and summer-dry climate. Most of our native trees with such leaves (e.g., cottonwood and alder) therefore grow near watercourses. Instead of making all of the leaves of the plant "suffer" from the drought, some of the leaves turn yellow and drop, leaving the available water to be distributed among the remaining leaves. Plants are smarter than we think.

But many drought-tolerant conifers shed their leaves, too. And that might lead you to believe that something is wrong with your tree. Should you water it? Should you fertilize it? Should you (gasp!) cut it down? None of the above. In most cases, you just need to let it alone. Most conifers are evergreens; that is, they retain at least some of their needles all year long. But *all* evergreen conifers lose their *oldest* needles once a year, typically in late summer and early fall. Coast redwoods, for example, shed their oldest branchlets—which have died and turned an attractive, reddish-brown color—in August and September. To passersby, the trees may look sick, but the redwoods are just doing what comes naturally. (Unlike pines, spruces, Douglas-firs, and many other conifers that shed individual needles, redwoods, sequoias, and "false" cedars—such as incense-cedar and Port-Orford-cedar—lose entire branchlets.)

If you need to sweep them off of walkways and driveways, they can make an attractive and useful mulch elsewhere in your yard or garden. But if you've designed your landscape wisely, most of the needles that fall can just be left where they lie. As they break down over time, their nutrients will be reused by the tree from which they fell. Meanwhile, they provide a wonderful and free mulch for both the tree and the other plants growing beneath it.

Broad-leafed evergreen trees also lose their oldest leaves once a year, typically in early to midsummer just after the new year's leaves have finished developing. Some gardeners find this habit very irksome because the leaves fall onto their neat beds of bark mulch, creating "litter" that simply *must* be raked out. Southern magnolias planted in the middle of manicured lawns create an almost insurmountable problem for some people because the trees lose their very large, leathery leaves over a period of many weeks in summer.

One way to solve this is to underplant broad-leafed and needle-leafed evergreen trees with appropriate groundcovers that can absorb this annual leaf fall without creating an untidy landscape. Unfortunately, our landscapes often seem designed to create work for us when, with a few adjustments, they could largely care for themselves.

Another way to view these leaf losses is to see them as marking the seasons. When the first branchlets begin falling from the redwoods, it must be August. A little later, in early fall, the area's ponderosa pines lose their older needles. There's always something going on in the natural world. Learn to delight in these interesting changes instead of seeing them as making work for you. You're likely to feel a lot better about gardening, and perhaps about yourself, too.

(This article first appeared in the Fall 2002 edition of *ETF News.*)

TREE LEAVES CAN BE BENEFICIAL
TO YARDS

ALL SUMMER LONG, while many of us humans are inside anxiously looking at our watches or staring at flickering computer screens, the leaves on broad-leafed deciduous trees are outside enjoying the sunshine and making the world a better place for all of us. But come fall, the party's over. Their work completed, they undergo a series of physiological changes brought on by the changing photoperiod (shorter days and longer nights). Their green chlorophyll breaks down, revealing whatever other pigments the abundant chlorophyll has masked all summer long. And here in the temperate zone, the Flaming Foliage Festival begins.

Green ashes turn yellow and sugar maples turn orange. Some trees lose their leaves while they're still green or after they turn brown; but green and brown are colors, too! And all the leaves come tumbling down, as they have for many thousands of autumns before this one.

Fallen leaves provide a variety of benefits for the trees they fell from and for a host of other critters. They provide an insulating blanket that protects sensitive plant roots—most of which grow just beneath the surface of the soil—from temperature extremes during the coming winter. They act as herbicides to effectively prevent the growth of weeds. And they absorb the impact of heavy winter rains, thus reducing soil compaction and erosion.

They provide homes for all kinds of insects that are essential to the health of any landscape. Some of those insects are an important food source for many ground-feeding birds that overwinter here. And as fallen leaves slowly decompose, they recycle almost all of their nutrients, so the tree can use them again. The list of benefits goes on and on.

Many (but not all) evergreen trees shed their oldest leaves in fall, too. Ponderosa pines, for example, carpet the ground with their beautiful needles. And the madrone (a *broad*-leafed evergreen tree) drops its oldest leaves.

But some deciduous trees just cannot seem to make up their minds in fall. Their leaves color up just like other leaves, but then they refuse to fall off the tree! Instead, they turn brown and remain on the tree as fall turns to winter. Pin oaks are one of the most common trees in our area that have delayed leaf drop. But other oaks (e.g., red, scarlet, English, and Oregon white) also exhibit this phenomenon, as do beeches, hornbeams, and sugar maples.

For leaves to fall off, an *abscission zone* (or layer of dead cells) must form at the base of the leaf's petiole or stalk. In trees with *marcescent* leaves, however, the abscission zone remains alive even after the leaf's blade and most of the petiole have died. The leaf thus has no choice but to hang on. Many marcescent leaves may be physically ripped off the tree during winter storms, but their petiole bases usually remain until spring, when the formation of the abscission zone is completed.

For some local landscape maintenance people and homeowners, marcescent leaves are seen as a real pain. After all the other leaves have fallen, here's this dribble of leaves that fall all winter long from the pin oaks. (They're only a pain, of course, if you insist on an ultra-tidy landscape.) The good news for these people is that marcescent leaves are a juvenile trait and trees eventually outgrow it. Older trees of species with marcescent leaves may indeed retain some of their leaves in the lower and inside portions of the canopy (the parts of the tree that developed during its youth), but the upper and outer portions will lose their leaves "on time."

Interestingly, a few of these trees are just plain precocious. The row of pin oaks on the west side of the exhibit halls at Lane County Fairgrounds, for example, includes one individual that has always lost *all* of its leaves in fall.

So if you wish to plant pin oaks (or sugar maples, etc.) that will lose all their leaves when *you* think they should, just visit a tree nursery sometime between late October and mid-November. Walk down the row of trees and select only those individuals that are already leafless (perhaps one out of every ten or twenty trees will meet this criterion). It's that easy.

If you feel that raking leaves, in general, is a hassle you'd rather not have, then perhaps you should consider redesigning your landscape a bit. Instead of trying to grow grass underneath trees, turn those areas into shrub beds and just let the leaves lie where they fall. If you do have small areas of lawn or paved surfaces that you must rake, incorporate those leaves into nearby shrub or vegetable beds. Make every effort, though, not to remove the leaves from your premises, because by doing so, you're removing important plant nutrients and depriving your landscape of all the other good things that leaves do.

Both our lives and our gardens are enriched by leaves. Let's get outside now and enjoy the season!

(This article first appeared in the 3 October 1997 edition of *Northeast Neighbor.*)

WILLAMETTE PLAZA TO GET TREES:
IT'S THE LAW!

FOR MANY YEARS, one of the top contenders in Eugene's Ugliest Parking Lot Contest has been the barren expanse at Willamette Plaza (near 29th and Willamette). But we are happy to announce that change is underway, and it is change for the better.

As part of the shopping center's redevelopment over the next couple of years—and its rebirth as the trendy Woodfield Station—the Eugene land use code requires that the parking lot "landscape" be brought up to current standards. That means the construction of planting beds at least six feet in width; the installation of automatic irrigation; and the planting of large-canopy trees as well as extensive understory plantings of shrubs and herbaceous plants such as ornamental grasses and flowers.

This site is an especially difficult one for tree growth because of the dense and poorly drained soil that underlies the existing parking lot. Compared to parking lots that sit atop deep, well-drained river loam (e.g., the Costco lot at Beltline and Coburg Road), where most trees grow vigorously and eventually should attain substantial size, the prognosis for the new trees at Woodfield Station is not good. Even though most of the tree species selected by the project's landscape architect are suited to poorly drained soils (red maples, ashes, European hornbeams), it is unlikely that they will ever develop into a magnificent leafy canopy covering the entire parking area, which is the goal of the city code.

One way that future site managers might help the new trees is by implementing a regular fertilization program that would provide the necessary nutrients for tree growth to supplement those available inside the planting area "pot" that most of the trees' roots will be confined to.

The new plantings will nonetheless be an enormous improvement over the desolate asphalt desert that has "welcomed" customers to the Willamette Plaza site for many decades. Hurray for the city planning staff who included these landscaping standards in the most recent update of Eugene's land use code!

Greenery always improves the scenery!

(This article first appeared in the March 2006 edition of *ETF News*.)

BE VERY CAREFUL ABOUT PLANTING LEYLAND-CYPRESS

SEVERAL YEARS AGO, my friend, Bob, came to me with a neighborhood problem that he thought I could solve. The apartment complex adjacent to his property had an unshielded light that shone onto his property and into his bedroom all night long. Repeated requests to the apartments' manager to adjust the light had been unsuccessful.

Bob thought that I might know of an evergreen plant that grew fast, as the offending light was at the roofline of the two-story apartment building. I was familiar with a plant used in Europe mostly for hedges that I thought would do the trick. At that time, the plant was still relatively uncommon in our area, yet I knew I could find some at a local nursery.

We decided to plant a short row of four of the plants to ensure that the light would not be seen anywhere on his property. The plants he purchased were quite small, but he had high hopes, so to speak, that within a few years, the plants would quickly grow tall enough to solve his problem with the light.

Bob was not disappointed. The first year, the plants grew nearly four feet and, indeed, within a short time, they were fifteen feet tall and performing their job very well. But he didn't want them to grow any taller than that, or they would block the sunlight from reaching his yard and all the sun-loving plants he and his wife grew there. And he didn't want them growing *laterally* out into the yard and consuming valuable space on his family's small lot.

To keep the plants at about fifteen feet in height and three to four feet in width, Bob now prunes them twice a year. And he will have to continue doing that until the day he or the plants die. Alas, by solving one problem, the light, we created another, since it is not very easy to prune something that is fifteen feet tall.

The plant I'd recommended to Bob is Leyland-cypress (X *Cupresso-cyparis leylandii*). It is an unusual hybrid between two different genera (or "genuses") of plants, hence the capital X preceding its genus name. One of its parents is the Monterey cypress (*Cupressus macrocarpa*), a vigorous and very horizontally branched conifer native to California's Monterey Peninsula that is planted widely elsewhere in the world, especially at seaside sites in the temperate zone. Its other parent is the Alaska yellow-cedar (*Chamaecyparis nootkatensis*), a more upright-growing conifer with attractive, pendulous branches that is native from Oregon's West Cascades up into Alaska and is sometimes planted in gardens.

This hybrid first occurred in Wales in 1888. Since then, a number of named cultivars (cultivated varieties) have been recognized, and it has been extensively planted in Europe. That's perhaps an understatement. Some horticulturists think that the tree has been greatly overplanted, and on many sites in Europe, it is causing problems due to its unanticipated vigor. In England, there are even websites devoted to this plant that warn unsuspecting gardeners what they are getting into if they plant Leyland-cypress.

The biggest problem is, well, how BIG the plant can get, and how fast. Particularly on sites with well-drained soil where the plants are watered and fertilized, they can quickly grow to gargantuan size. In many European gardens where these trees were originally planted as "fast-growing hedges" they soon overwhelmed their owners, who tired of the regular pruning and allowed the plants to engulf not just their own little backyards, but the backyards of their neighbors as well.

In our area, Leyland-cypress is being planted with increasing frequency on commercial sites where there is sometimes enough space for it to develop its huge canopy. But it's also becoming popular with homeowners for that "quick screen" and I cringe at the thought. Because few of us are familiar with the plant, since it's still somewhat uncommon around here, we may be duped into planting something we later regret. Who would imagine that such a pretty little conifer in a one-gallon pot at the garden center could become a monster?

But it can. So buyer beware. There is nothing "wrong" with Leyland-cypress, but know what you're getting into if you're considering planting it. Take a cue from our friends, the Brits, where some people have gone so far as to declare war on Leyland-cypresses, and neighbor-against-neighbor lawsuits over the plants are not uncommon.

(This article first appeared in the 7 May 2003 edition of *The Springfield News*.)

TREES FOR COMMERCIAL DISTRICTS

MANY BUSINESS OWNERS recognize the important economic and environmental benefits that trees and other vegetation can provide for them, for their customers, and for their community. But they are sometimes hesitant to plant trees—or come to regret their decision after trees are planted—due to misconceptions about how trees grow and develop over time.

Understandably, many businesses are concerned with the visibility of their building, their display windows, and their signs. A common refrain one hears when recommending that trees be planted in a commercial area is, "That's fine, as long as they won't block my signs." Often, owners insist that only "small" trees be planted in an effort to meet their primary criterion. But small-canopy trees, by their very nature, are likely to cause more visibility problems than larger-canopy trees ever would.

Indeed, as smaller-canopy trees mature, they can completely obscure the view of an adjacent building. And efforts to maintain visibility are invariably directed at the trees, whose canopies are then topped or "gumdropped" in an attempt to control their growth. But such severe pruning is not only an extra expense and a maintenance headache. It often results in even denser growth low in the canopy, thus exacerbating the problem. Eventually, the owner comes to resent the trees altogether and they are finally removed.

The loss of trees in such instances is tragic enough, especially where they probably won't be replanted for a long time. But more importantly, our community sometimes loses a one-time tree advocate when, with a little bit of forethought, the whole sorry mess could have been avoided.

Business owners need to carefully weigh the benefits and drawbacks of planting trees near their businesses. And they need to recognize that, at least when young, *any* tree will reduce building visibility to some degree. But with proper selection of individual planting sites and species, it is always possible to incorporate trees while at the same time maintaining superior visibility.

The most successful way to have trees and good business, too, is to plant a *small* number of *large*-canopy trees, rather than a large number of small-canopy trees. Over time, the former can have their lower limbs removed, until their canopies are completely up and "out of the way." Such an approach eventually results in an elevated canopy that provides both welcome shade and an attractive setting, making the business even more appealing to customers and passersby.

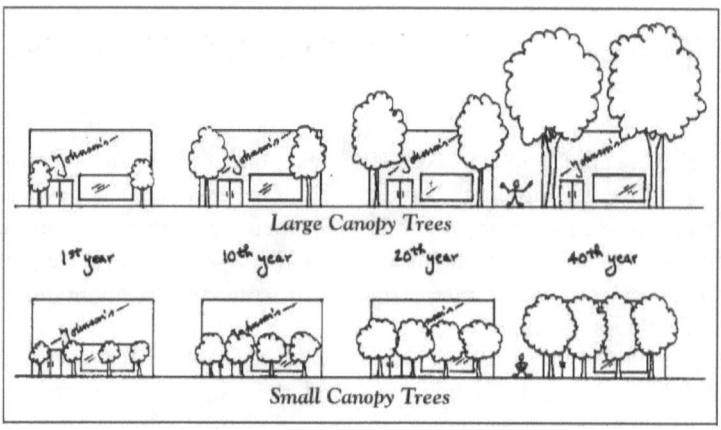

(This article first appeared in the Summer 2005 edition of *ETF News*.)

CONVERTING DENDROPHOBES

ONE OF MY MOST DIFFICULT TASKS as a tree advocate is listening to the reasons some people have for not liking trees. The trees will block their business's sign; the seed pods are slippery to walk on; the roots will crack the sidewalk; the shade is unwanted; the leaves are too big or too plentiful to rake; and on and on. Some people, I am persuaded, are just born to complain.

This past summer, as I met with neighbors along Harris Street to encourage them to water the trees that ETF and neighborhood volunteers planted last winter, the response was overwhelmingly positive. As usual, however, there were The Complainers. Some of these people, of course, "didn't want any trees in the first place." And here I was asking them to water those very trees, what nerve!

I explained that the City of Eugene's water trucks could water the trees for the entire summer at a cost to taxpayers of about $100 per tree. Or the neighbors themselves could water them for about 15 cents a tree. If they still balked, I offered to water the trees myself if they would just let me hook up my hose to their faucet once a week.

One neighbor wouldn't even accept that. She insisted that she simply wouldn't be able to pay her water bill if I used her faucet. "Here's a dollar," I said to her, "to more than cover the cost of the water I'll use this summer." No, she didn't want any part of my suspicious scheme. So I asked an adjacent neighbor if I could use his faucet to water her two trees, which he was happy to agree to.

Several weeks later, when I arrived to water the young woman's trees, I noticed that someone had already done it. Hmm. Then the next week, as I approached on my bicycle, I saw to my astonishment The Complainer herself watering the trees in the park strip and weeding around them. Aha! I stopped to chat, being careful not to mention our earlier, less-than-pleasant conversation. She was very talkative and went out of her way to show me how she had cared for her newly planted catalpas, and how much it upset her when passersby would leave litter near the trees.

I could scarcely conceal my glee over her change of heart! I had witnessed the complete conversion of an outspoken dendrophobe (tree hater) into a gentle and protective dendrophile in a period of just a few weeks. That's one of the best parts of being a tree advocate: watching someone reconnect for whatever reasons with the trees around us. I pedaled back home with a grin that stretched halfway around my head!

(This article first appeared in the Fall 1999 edition of *ETF News*.)

TIMELY PRUNING OF TREES A NECESSITY

PROPER AND TIMELY PRUNING of young trees can significantly reduce the cost of maintaining those trees as they grow older. Good pruning can also reduce the potential for "tree failures"—for example, breaking or splitting of branches—as trees mature.

Over the past decade, Eugene's wonderful NeighborWoods program has made possible the planting of many hundreds of young trees in the public right-of-way around our community. Even trees that are healthy and well pruned when they arrive from the nursery sometimes require help during their first years to establish strong leaders (or trunks) and laterals (side branches).

Eugene's Parks and Open Space staff recognize this need, but have been unable to provide the necessary care. Because of staff reductions, Eugene now has only one tree crew, consisting of three people, to care for the tens of thousands of maturing and mature trees that line our streets. Some of the work (e.g., tree removals) is contracted out, but there is just no staff time available for the pruning of young trees.

ETF strives to maintain the young trees that our own volunteers have planted over the past five years. And we continue to plant more without any real assurance that we, or city staff, will be able to guide them properly through their youth and into healthy adulthood.

Recently, ETF board members Phil Carroll and Whitey Lueck performed major reconstructive surgery on pin oaks at the northeast corner of 13th and Adams—across from the county fairgrounds—and in front of Berg's Ski Shop at 13th and Lawrence. At both sites, neighbors had repeatedly mispruned the young trees, so recovery will take several years. But the prognosis is very good. The oaks at the northwest corner of East 18th Avenue and High Street, for example, had been "lollipopped" for years until Whitey's Lane Community College pruning class "operated" on them in 1990. Stop by some time to see how well they've recovered.

Fortunately, such severe cases of mispruning are relatively uncommon. Still, what about the thousands of young trees in our community that require attention? ETF hopes to persuade city councilors and others of the need for this essential pruning so that funds are procured to provide the service.

Meanwhile, ETF is looking into putting together a flyer or booklet to help homeowners properly prune new trees in their park strips and yards. Just as relatively inexpensive childhood immunizations prevent expensive and perhaps life-threatening problems later, so the pruning of young trees more than pays for itself in the long run.

(This article first appeared in the Spring 2003 edition of *ETF News.*)

OAKWAY TULIP-TREES COME DOWN

SOMETIME IN THE MID-1960s, some forward-thinking person or group of people planted 19 tulip-trees (*Liriodendron tulipifera*) in the publicly owned park strip along the east side of Oakway Road. Like other trees on the deep, fertile, well-drained river loam common to much of the so-called Ferry Street Bridge area of Eugene, the tulip-trees prospered, becoming in just four decades a magnificent neighborhood presence and a real attribute to the developing commercial area now called Oakway Center.

But the trees' phenomenal vigor—usually a laudable trait—was what eventually led to them being cut down. For many years, the adjacent property owners had repeatedly replaced the sidewalks that were lifted by the trees' growing roots. And City of Eugene Public Works staff adjusted and re-adjusted the thickness of the adjacent curbs and pavement, and the gravel base beneath them, to accommodate the growing roots.

In 2004, five of the trees were removed after being identified as potentially hazardous. That is, the city's urban forestry staff inspected the 19 trees and found sufficient reason (i.e., decay) in the trunk or at the base of the tree to warrant the removal of five of them. After that, the remaining 14 trees just continued doing what comes naturally: leafing out each spring; flowering in May; providing a lush green canopy all summer long; then turning golden in October and dropping their leaves.

However, as the street-side roots of the remaining trees began to raise more extensive areas of pavement, stormwater drainage from the street was disrupted, creating pools of water that were potentially hazardous to both cyclists and motorists. Public Works staff determined that the only way for stormwater to properly drain would be if the trees' large street-side roots were removed. Although the 14 trees were not yet "hazardous" trees, they would *become* hazardous if any large roots were cut on the upwind side of the huge trees. The trees were thus declared "nuisance" trees because of the irremediable problems their roots were causing to the pavement, and signs were posted in early fall of 2005 to inform passersby of the trees' proposed removal.

Few Eugeneans are aware of the long-term effort—by both city staff and the adjacent property owners—to save these wonderful trees. The City of Eugene does not cut down trees growing in the public right-of-way without good reason. There are many examples around our community where curbs have been moved, sidewalks relocated, and other steps taken to preserve existing trees if the trees are in good health and do not interfere with the use of the street.

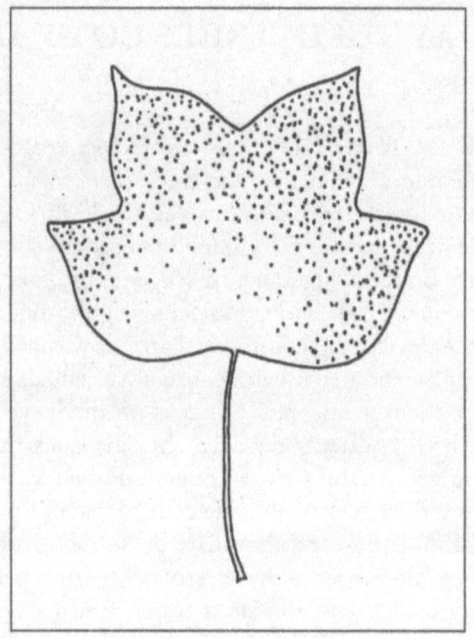

Tulip-tree leaf.

If the adjacent street pavement had been parking space instead of a travel lane, the outcome might have been different. But Oakway Road is a "minor arterial" with four lanes (and a central turn pocket) for motorized vehicles and two for bicycles. It was not possible to eliminate the eastern-most travel lane(s) in that busy commercial area.

The park strip that was once graced by the lovely tulip-trees will not be vacant for long. New large-canopy trees will be planted next fall or winter. Their roots will reach down into that wonderful river loam and their canopies will soon rise skyward. It would be appropriate if at least some of the trees were Oregon white oaks—the "signature" tree of that neighborhood and of Oakway Center's award-winning Heritage Courtyard. Bigleaf maple, another Oregon native that does best on river loam and is on the city's Approved Street Tree List, would also be perfectly suited to the site. Ideally, two or three different species of long-lived, large-canopy trees would make that stretch of Oakway Road once again a pleasant place to be, instead of the current "hole in the sky" where once the tulip-trees raised their lofty crowns.

Because the park strip will be treeless throughout the coming summer and into fall, the City and the adjacent property owners might consider placing little signs—atop attractive, sturdy, painted posts—where each of the new trees will be planted. A typical sign could say: "Coming in fall 2006: A bigleaf maple." And the next time a group of large, healthy trees needs to be removed elsewhere in Eugene, a large sign explaining in detail (and including illustrations) why the removals are necessary would help passersby understand how the decision was made, and go a long way toward educating Eugeneans about the trials and tribulations of being an urban tree.

(This article first appeared in the May 2006 edition of *ETF News*.)

MANAGING OUR FORESTS

THERE HAS BEEN A LOT OF DISCUSSION in the past ten to twenty years about how we should log forested parcels that are managed primarily for timber production. Participants in this sometimes very lively dialogue have included foresters, the general public, soil scientists, forest biologists, owners of timbered land (both public and private), and many others. As a result, there have been substantial changes in how we look at forested land in general and, more specifically, how we care for individual sites. These changes have been driven by a variety of factors, including aesthetics, forest ecology, and economics.

From the end of World War II until the 1990s, most forested sites west of the Cascade crest were treated similarly when they were logged. All the large, sound logs from the site were hauled off to the mill. Snags (standing dead trees) were cut and, along with rotting logs from the stand, were piled and burned. The entire site was then burned to remove the slash (branches cut from the felled trees) to clear the site and prepare for replanting with Douglas-fir.

But these days, on both public and private forest lands, the so-called prescriptions for how individual sites will be managed can vary greatly. A south-facing slope—that gets hotter and drier in summer—may be treated differently than a north-facing one. Sites with streams running through them are managed differently than sites without streams. A forested stand in a scenic corridor may be selectively logged or logging may be prohibited altogether. Steep slopes, too, may be off-limits to logging.

On flatter ground, machinery with fat, low-pressure tires may be permitted on the site. On hillier sites, logs must be partially or fully suspended from a cable before removal, to protect the soil. Some snags may be left because of their value to wildlife, and slash may go unburned or be gathered into piles before burning.

For most of us, our opinions of forest management in general, and logging in particular, are based on what we can see from our vehicles as we cross through the Coast Range on our way to Florence or through the West Cascades on our way to Bend. We may see distant clearcuts and complain about how awful they look. Or we might peek through narrow roadside buffers of standing trees to see the "ravaged landscape" beyond. As far as we can tell from a car moving at 55 miles per hour, the proverbial glass is half empty and getting emptier by the minute.

Most of the good things that are going on in forestry are located well away from the paved roads and few of us wander very far from the main highways. So when a stand of timber near a main highway is treated in a way that merits attention, it's an opportunity we shouldn't pass up.

About two years ago, a forested site owned by Rosboro Lumber Co., based here in Springfield, was logged right next to the McKenzie Highway, and hardly anyone noticed. (The site is just west of milepost 19 and the Eugene Water and Electric Board powerhouse for the Leaburg power canal.) Although most of the trees were removed from the site and hauled off to the mill, many were not.

Some passersby may prefer to look at the site, focus on the stumps, and rant about how we humans continue to ruin what was at one time a really nice planet. But let's look beyond the stumps to see what was done differently here. In addition to the large conifers that remain, many broad-leafed trees (e.g., bigleaf maple) were also left. Some of the slash was piled and burned, but extensive areas of the site were not burned at all. And the site was replanted with unusually large Douglas-fir seedlings, some of them almost waist-high, in an effort to re-green this well-traveled corridor as soon as possible. Other species such as western redcedar and grand fir were planted, too, where appropriate.

Sure, the site still looks pretty roughed up compared to a pristine stand of 80-year-old trees. But let's keep an eye on it. Over the next few years, the spindly maples will develop broader canopies now that they're out in the sun, and the young firs will take off and quickly fill in most of the area. Meanwhile, the tall firs that were not cut will help the new firs get established by shading this hot, south-facing slope during part of the day. And, of course, the slash that was not burned helps mulch the ground, keeping it cooler and moister and reducing erosion.

Because this site is adjacent to an important and scenic highway, it might have had a buffer strip of uncut trees left right along the road. But due to the proximity of EWEB lines and the possibility that some of the trees might topple onto the lines after their neighbors were removed, the buffer strip was eliminated. In a way, I'm glad that it was. Now we have an unimpeded view of a parcel of forested land that, for a variety of good reasons, is being managed in a much more sensitive way than we used to do.

In my humble opinion, the glass is decidedly half full.

(This article first appeared in the 29 March 2003 edition of
The Springfield News.)

LATE WINTER IS THE BEST TIME
TO PLANT TREES

I N LATE WINTER, I OFTEN GO TO BED with sore shoulders and a slightly aching back. It's a seasonal affliction that has nothing, however, to do with the weather. Rather, late winter is the ideal time of year to plant trees, and I tend to approach the task with so much gusto that, well, I simply overdo it.

That's easy to do. Tree planting is an immensely satisfying activity whether one is planting a single tree or reforesting a hillside. And everywhere west of the Cascades just naturally wants to grow trees.

Although one can plant trees year round in our area, the dormant season is by far the best time. That way, the trees can get settled in their new home before spring arrives. Wintertime planting also permits the use of bare-root trees, which are less expensive than containerized trees and balled-and-burlapped trees, and are so much easier to handle.

Local nurseries and garden centers sell most fruit trees bare root, but you sometimes have to shop around to find other trees such as ash and maple bare root. Still, it's worth it to find bare-root trees because it's hard work digging and backfilling the hole for a new tree; if you can be spared lifting a heavy ball of soil down into the hole, so much the better.

Some trees, however, simply do not lend themselves to bare-root transplanting, so they must be moved with soil around their roots. Examples include dogwoods, magnolias, tulip-trees, and sweetgums. But they are exceptions and not the rule.

When deciding what kind of tree to plant and where to plant it, there are several important things to consider. First, what kind of soil does your site have? If it is poorly drained clay, that limits the selection of trees that will do well there to ashes, a few of the maples (e.g., red and silver), and some other trees that naturally grow in poorly drained areas, such as sweetgums and pin oaks. But if your soil is well-drained river loam or you live in a hillier area, chances are you can plant almost any tree species that is cold-hardy in our area.

Second, what do you want and need the tree to "do?" Will it be just an ornamental landscape feature, or do you want it to work for a living? I prefer working trees myself; that is, trees that perform a variety of functions in addition to being pretty. One function is *environmental modification*, where you plant trees to block the wind, for example, or to shade the west side of your house in summer. You might also consider the *ecological* functions of the tree. Trees native to this area perform far more ecological services to local plant and animal communities, for instance, than trees that come from other parts of the world.

Third, is there room for the tree to develop without interfering with utility wires or a building or a neighbor's view? There is no sight sadder than a tree that was planted in the wrong place and then was given a crewcut because it "got too big." Trees don't get too big; they just do what they are genetically programmed to do. If you need a tree that will never get more than twenty feet tall, then plant that kind of tree rather than a Douglas-fir or a bigleaf maple.

When you are ready to plant your tree, choose a day when it's not raining and avoid stepping on the soil in the planting area itself. These precautions help preserve what is called *soil structure* and help ensure that your new tree will grow well.

Dig a hole just deep enough to accommodate the tree's roots or root ball; it's always better to plant the tree a little high than to plant it too deep. But dig the hole so it is about half again as wide as the root mass or root ball. Then break up the soil clods the best you can, and backfill the hole. Again, do not tramp on the soil around the new tree or compact it with your shovel. Rather, water the new tree well, even if the soil is already wet. Water and gravity together will carry smaller soil particles down and around the tree's roots, filling in any little air pockets that might remain after planting.

Most new trees do not need to be staked, despite what you see everywhere on newly landscaped commercial sites. If, however, the tree begins to lean a few days or weeks after planting, then you can go back and place two stakes on opposite sides of the trunk, each about 18 inches from the trunk. Tie the tree to the stakes with thick, soft rope, but never with wire or cord that can cut into the tree's bark or cause other problems. Tie the tree as low as 18 to 24 inches from the ground to permit adequate tree movement that will ensure good trunk development.

The first year after planting, most trees "sleep" and grow very little. The second year, they "creep," growing a bit more but not quite at full speed yet. Finally, the third year after planting, they "leap." By then, they should be completely recovered from the shock of transplanting and on their way to becoming healthy adults.

In our area, all young trees need supplemental water during their three-year establishment period. Even native trees need summer water, unless they are just one- or two-year-old conifer seedlings. So remember that young trees, just like children, are depending on you for a little help until they can handle life on their own.

If you already have all the trees you want and need on your property, consider helping a neighbor plant a few trees. Or write a letter to your local supermarket and propose that they plant some trees to bring life to their otherwise barren parking lot.

As well-treed as parts of our communities already are, there are still plenty of opportunities for tree planting. The only reason that wonderful, old trees shade many of our streets and homes these days is because someone planted them 50 or 75 years ago. Now it's our turn to plant the trees that future generations will enjoy. Satisfaction guaranteed.

(This article first appeared in the 21 February 2001 edition of
The Springfield News.)

A COMPARISON OF LEAF REMOVAL
PROGRAMS IN SIX COMMUNITIES

FOR THOUSANDS OF YEARS here in the middle latitudes, deciduous broad-leafed trees have dropped their leaves every fall, just like clockwork. The natural leaf mulch that developed beneath the trees maintained a rich habitat for a host of critters, from invertebrates to birds and small mammals. Over time, the leaves decomposed and returned their nutrients to the soil, to be used again by the tree that produced them, in a cycle that was both simple and elegant.

Eventually, towns and cities arose in which people planted trees, first for food, and more recently for both shade and ornament. Meanwhile, mowed lawns became fashionable, and leaves that fell on the lawns needed to be removed so they didn't smother the grass. Leaves also needed to be removed from the roofs of buildings, as well as from paved areas such as sidewalks and streets. Generally, leaves that were removed were not re-distributed near the site where they fell—to recycle their nutrients and provide all the other benefits of fallen leaves—but were either burned or removed from the site and dumped in a landfill.

These days, for environmental reasons, the burning of leaves is prohibited in most communities, and leaves are no longer hauled to landfills. Most people deal with the leaves that fall from trees growing on their own properties and in the adjacent publicly owned park strip (if any) by having them hauled off-site—despite strong encouragement from municipalities to compost the leaves on-site or use them as mulch.

Since the 1960s, Eugene has had a fall leaf collection program that removes leaves that have been placed in the street for pickup—leaves that have fallen both on the adjacent *private* property as well as those that have fallen in the *public* right-of-way (sidewalk, park strip, and street). And

132

Eugene rightly boasts that, these days, all of the leaves that are picked up are "recycled" in one of three ways: 1) by being delivered to residents who request the leaves and use them as mulch or compost material; 2) by being taken to community gardens; and 3) by being composted by commercial recyclers or used on city parkland.

Eugeneans are asked to place leaves to be picked up in the street *no sooner than the weekend before their scheduled pickup*, so they don't block the street, bike lanes, or curbside parking areas, and so they don't create stormwater problems due to blocked gutters and storm drains. And the city maintains an excellent website showing the real-time status of the leaf removal program, including where crews are currently working and where they'll be headed next.

The clogging of storm drains or catch basins is just one of the many problems that fallen leaves can cause if they are not removed from the street properly and promptly.

But the fact is that most Eugeneans ignore the rules and place their leaves in the street long before pickup begins. They do this for the simple reason that they don't have anywhere on their properties to *store* the leaves until pickup week, and they don't want to have to move the leaves twice, once to a storage area and later to the street.

Unlike areas with more continental climates east of the Cascades, where the leaves come tumbling down over a period of sometimes just two or three weeks, fall is a long, drawn-out affair here in the maritime Northwest. The first trees to lose their leaves in Eugene (mostly ash species) begin to drop them in late September and early October. By the end of October, many other deciduous trees have dropped their leaves, as well, but there are still more to come in November. Eugene's public works crews generally don't even begin picking up leaves until mid-November or later. In the meantime, the leaves piled in the streets by residents cause a variety of problems—from creating a safety issue for pedestrians and cyclists, to clogging storm drains—despite the best efforts of city staff to prevent those problems.

Eventually, sometime in January most years, Eugene's streets are largely cleared of leaves, following the expenditure of an enormous amount of time, labor, and fossil fuels to remove and "re-distribute" the leaves. These days, the leaf removal program is funded by stormwater fees that every city property owner pays. Most people think the program works well, and of course everyone is happy once the streets have been cleared. But is there possibly a better way?

In preparing this article, the leaf programs of five other municipalities were examined, including four here in the Willamette Valley—Springfield, Corvallis, Salem, and Portland—as well as one out-of-state program in Loveland, Colorado. Interestingly, but perhaps not surprisingly, no two of the six programs were alike. Every community has its own way of dealing with fallen leaves, and every person interviewed felt that his or her program works well.

All six communities recycle or compost their leaves—to keep them from ending up in the local landfill. Some cities have fairly simple systems and rules to follow regarding leaf removal; others are quite complicated. One of the biggest differences among the six cities, however, regards how they treat leaves that fall on *private* property versus those that fall on *public* property.

In Eugene, for instance, there is no distinction. All leaves placed in the street are picked up, regardless of where they came from. The situation is identical in Corvallis and Portland. In Springfield, crews collect leaves from private property but *only* if they are put into plastic trash sacks and placed curbside for pickup by the local waste hauler (for eventual composting).

In both Salem and Loveland, it is the responsibility of the property owner to remove the leaves that have fallen on their own property as well as those on the publicly owned park strips between curb and sidewalk that are by law maintained by adjacent property owners in most communities. Salem and Loveland then use street sweepers and other machinery to remove only those leaves that have fallen onto the street. And both Salem and Loveland have free drop-off sites where residents can haul the leaves from their properties themselves and at their own expense. (Those leaves are then composted by the municipality.)

Among the cities that accept leaves from both private and public property—other than Springfield and its bag-your-own program—there are also differences. Eugene generally makes two sweeps through each neighborhood, one in November/December and one in January, and the program is funded by stormwater fees, as mentioned above. Corvallis's waste hauler picks up leaves placed in the street weekly (!) during the fall, and the cost of the program is included in all Corvallis residents' monthly fee for trash collection.

Okay, are you ready for the next example? In Portland, the parts of the city where there are "high concentrations of mature trees"—which are scattered throughout the city—are divided into 30 "leaf removal zones," 18 of which are serviced twice in fall, and 12 just once. Residents in the leaf removal zones must pay an annual fee of $15–30 ($5–10 for low-income residents) for leaf removal, but they may "opt out" of the program either by assuring the City that they will be providing all leaf removal themselves, or by having no trees in their yards or along the street that can drop leaves into the street. If a resident wishes to opt out, however, there is first an opt-out application to complete. That leads to an opt-out evaluation, which may result in an opt-out approval and notification—unless, of course, the application is denied. If it's denied, there is still the possibility of filing an opt-out appeal. (Oh, and by the way, Portland residents who do succeed in getting an opt-out approval must apply *annually* for a leaf removal program opt out "because conditions change.") Any questions about how this little program works? Whew!

Leaves that are left in the street where they are repeatedly run over by cars become a real hazard and are difficult to remove.

Although the supervisors of all six programs say they are content with how things work overall in their respective communities, an outside observer might well reach another conclusion. Some programs appear far more efficient at getting the job of leaf removal done than others do. Of those communities that accept leaves from private property— Eugene, Springfield, Corvallis, and Portland—Corvallis's system appears to work the best (again, *weekly* pickup is provided by the local waste hauler for a fee that is included in the monthly waste-hauling fee).

The supervisors of the leaf removal programs in Salem and Loveland both agreed that permitting residents to place leaves from their own properties—and from the park strips in front of their properties—into the street for pickup by the municipality amounts to a significant and unfair subsidy. Homeowners who choose to manage their own leaves by using them on-site or by paying someone to haul them off end up subsidizing those homeowners who, for whatever reasons, just push their leaves out into the street.

In some communities—but not in Eugene—it is illegal to pile leaves in the street.

Of course, in Portland, homeowners who receive an opt-out approval don't pay any fee and therefore do not directly subsidize the leaf removal program. But the approval itself comes at a cost, both to the property owner who takes the time every year to apply for it, as well as, surely, to the municipality that administers the complex program.

There may indeed be no perfect approach to leaf removal. But after examining the programs in these six communities, it appears that Salem and Loveland—where the municipality is responsible for removing the leaves that fall onto *public* property (the street) and property owners are responsible for removing the leaves from their *private* properties as well as the park strips at their own expense—have the most efficient, equitable, and simple programs for leaf removal. Just some food for thought for the other four cities in this survey.

(This article first appeared in the Winter 2013 newsletter of *Friends of Trees*.)

WINTER-BLOOMING TREES

MANY PEOPLE HAVE THE IMPRESSION that, during the winter, trees—especially broad-leafed deciduous ones—are completely dormant, or at least they won't be producing flowers until the longer and warmer days of spring. But thanks to relatively mild winters here in western Oregon, it's possible to find at least one species of broad-leafed tree—and sometimes several or more—in bloom during any given month of winter.

In December, the long, dangling, pollen-bearing catkins of European filberts begin to develop—and the tiny, magenta female flowers do, too, though they're not nearly as conspicuous. And in January, we begin to see the first elm flowers. Yes, you have to look closely, but you certainly don't need a microscope to see their flowers.

Red maple (Acer rubrum) *typically flowers in February in Eugene.*

Most of the trees that bloom during the winter have relatively inconspicuous flowers that are wind-pollinated. But trees with showier and insect-pollinated flowers—such as the earliest magnolias and some of the flowering cherries and plums—are already in bloom some years in mid-February or definitely by March, which is of course still "winter."

Sometimes, the flowers of winter-blooming broad-leafed trees are killed during one of our occasional cold snaps. But many of these trees produce their flowers over a period of several weeks so that, even if some of the flowers are killed by cold, others won't be. And even if all of the flowers happen to be killed one year by extreme cold, there's always next year, since trees are long-lived perennial plants that will have multiple opportunities to reproduce during their lifetimes.

So get outside and take a closer look at what's happening in the world around us. There are signs of spring everywhere, even if it's only early February!

(This article first appeared in the Winter 2010 edition of *ETF News*.)

BIGLEAF MAPLE FLOWERS: EUGENE'S HARBINGER OF SPRING

ONE OF THE LOVELIEST SIGNS that spring has returned once again here in the southern Willamette Valley is the appearance of long, pendent clusters of yellow-green flowers on the bigleaf maples in local riparian and upland forests, as well as along Eugene's streets. But with so many other "showier" trees with "prettier" flowers coming into bloom at about the same time—saucer magnolias, Japanese flowering cherries, dogwoods, and others—our exuberant maple friends are sometimes forgotten, or even ignored.

Some of us, however, find it hard to ignore a tree that merits so many superlatives. The bigleaf maple is the *largest*-growing maple species in the world. It has the *biggest* leaves of any of the maples. It is one of the *most drought-tolerant* maples known. And no other maple bears such long, voluptuous clusters of flowers. What is there to ignore?

Although most of us these days use the adjective bigleaf to specify this maple, it also is sometimes called *broad-leaf* maple. But my favorite name of all—which it truly deserves—is Oregon maple. Western Oregon is about the middle of this species' natural range, which extends from coastal British Columbia to southern California. And Oregon is also home to the "champion" bigleaf maple in the entire world, an absolutely huge tree located near Jewell, in the Coast Range west of Portland.

If you happen to miss peak maple bloom here in the Eugene area—because, for example, you had to spend the entire month of April inside a dark closet—it is still possible to catch "the big show" at higher elevations in the West Cascades well into the month of May.

So, no excuses! Get out there and gaze upward into the gorgeous canopy of the biggest maple tree you can find, and just drool over its beauty. It will thank you for the attention by creating wonderful shade all summer, producing oxygen, providing homes for wildlife, and all the other wonderful things that really big trees do for us so much better than small trees.

The pendent flower clusters of bigleaf maple appear on Eugene's trees in early April—as well as on the cover of this book!

(This article first appeared in the Spring 2011 edition of *ETF News.*)

PRESCIENT PARENTS

I N AN EFFORT TO ENGAGE THE STUDENTS in my Trees
Across Oregon course at the University of Oregon, I often pass tree-
related items around the classroom so the students can see, touch, and
even smell the items. One day, it might be the hefty seed cone of a Coulter
pine. Another day, it could be a stick that a beaver has de-barked to eat the
nutritious cambium layer just beneath the bark. Or 50-million-year-old
fossilized dawn-redwood leaves from central Oregon. It means so much
more to the students to see these things up close than it would if I just
projected images on the screen, or drew sketches on the blackboard.

Most of the objects I pass around have a special meaning to me. I
acquired the pinecone during a field class I taught in the San Gabriel
Mountains of southern California in the late 1980s. The beaver stick I came
across while exploring along the Willamette River right in Eugene. The
dawn-redwood fossil was given to me by a neighbor boy who, with his
family, had visited the town of Fossil, Oregon—yes, there really is such a
place—where they dug for fossils in a hillside adjacent to the local high
school and happened to come across several fine specimens.

But perhaps the most valuable and meaning-filled possession of mine
that I pass around is a little book called *The Golden Nature Guide to Trees*. It
was given to me by my parents for my eighth birthday. I'm sure I looked at
it now and again through my youth, and into my Boy Scout years, but then
I forgot about it. Many years later, I came across the book when going
through things at my parents' house, and I brought it back with me to
Oregon.

Just inside the cover is inscribed, in my mother's handwriting: *To
Dennis Lueck—8 yrs old—July 9, 1960, from Daddy and Mother*. Little could
they have known that, one day, I'd be teaching a course about trees at the
university. Or was there in fact something about me that led them to

141

believe I'd find the book useful, and maybe want to know more someday about the trees that grew all around us? But they never gave tree books to any of my siblings. Why not? What was it about me that was different?

At that time, we lived in the small town of Jersey Shore in the mountains of north-central Pennsylvania. (The word Pennsylvania actually means Penn's Woods—after the family of the state's Quaker founder, William Penn—because it was once almost 100 percent forested.) I recall a childhood where we were free to roam, unlike many of today's children, and I roamed far and wide, at least within the hilltop neighborhood where we lived. Between our house and the high school at the bottom of the hill was a woods, where I spent much time. I also was constantly on the lookout for nesting birds, and during the breeding season from mid-spring to mid-summer, knew where most of the bird nests were within a two-hundred-yard radius of our house. I explored mostly on my own and of course climbed trees, when necessary, to peer into nests I'd spotted from the ground.

My siblings also spent time outside, but I don't think that my parents considered any of them especially interested in nature. I was evidently the sole "nature boy" and how I ended up like this, I suppose I'll never really know. But my love for the outdoors, whatever its source, was clearly nurtured by my parents, and the tree book—as well as many other gifts through the years—is evidence of that.

More than fifty years later, in the community where I chose to make my home, many people refer to me as "the tree guy"—even though I maintain that I am a "whole" person and not just a tree guy. During my early years of underemployment in Eugene, I spent countless hours bicycling the streets and alleys and looking at the trees. I was especially interested in the less commonly planted trees and rejoiced whenever I stumbled upon one. And I have always been fascinated to think about how trees came to grow where they do. Every tree, like every person, has a story to tell. Unfortunately, trees can't talk—or perhaps we just don't yet know how to understand what they've been trying to tell us for so long.

Over the years, though, I've discovered the stories of many of our local trees by talking with my elders and by poring over old photographs, and I enjoy telling others what I've found. From 1987–1998, I researched and led monthly "tree walks" between April and November, where attendees and I would explore a Eugene neighborhood's trees—a different neighborhood each month. It became quite a social event for many people and something they looked forward to. Attendance probably averaged about 50 people, but I recall one tour in the South University Neighborhood where there were 116 tree lovers along. That was a bit unwieldy, but people seemed to have a good time nonetheless.

I've planted and overseen the planting of hundreds of trees around Eugene over the years, and I've often found myself publicly advocating for their preservation when "development" threatened. A few times I was successful; many times I was not. But each time I said something in defense of trees, I planted another seed in someone's mind about the benefits and wonders of trees, and that ripple effect is far more important in the long run than the preservation of an individual tree.

In 1997, I cofounded Eugene Tree Foundation—now Friends of Trees—and for more than a decade I wrote most of the lead articles for the organization's quarterly newsletter and served as its editor. And I have worked with City of Eugene urban forestry staff to improve the quality of care that trees around the community receive.

Besides teaching "the trees class" at the university, I continue to advocate for trees. Most recently, I took a stand in defiance of University planners who elected to remove one of the largest and oldest London plane-trees in Oregon, just so the campus student union could be enlarged. I give a half-dozen campus tree tours every year to both public and private groups, and I continue to plant and care for trees both on my own property and in my neighborhood.

Regardless of how my parents knew so long ago that this was the path down which I'd one day walk, it's a path I've enjoyed walking along for several decades now. And since my parents are no longer living, it doesn't look like I'll ever again receive another little book—on a different subject—that might risk diverting my attention from this path I so dearly love.

(This essay first appeared in *Staying Put in Lane County*,
my first collection of essays, published in 2015.)

CITY WORKS TO PROTECT
ESTABLISHED TREES

THE PROTECTION AND PRESERVATION of our city's trees occur at many different levels, both literally and figuratively. In terms of the trees themselves, it is important to care properly for all the parts of the tree, including those parts that are aboveground—the crown or canopy, and the trunk—as well as the roots that are mostly hidden from view. And with regard to the people who care for our trees, they can range from a thoughtful neighbor who removes a yard-sale sign nailed to the trunk of a young tree, to our city's urban forestry technicians who oversee the care of trees during construction and development.

What happens to trees' canopies and trunks is apparent to most observant passersby. But what happens to trees' roots, especially during construction and development, goes largely unnoticed, unless a person happens to be there the day the backhoe meets the roots, so to speak.

The summer 2006 reconstruction of Hilyard Street between East 13th Avenue and East 24th Avenue is illustrative of some of the good work that goes on behind the scenes (and underground) to protect Eugene's trees. Before the reconstruction work even began, all the street-side trees along the project's entire length were inventoried and each tree's Critical Root Zone (based on trunk diameter) was established. For some of the larger trees, such as two coast redwoods in the 1600 block, the CRZ was substantial and extended well out into the street.

In order to determine the actual extent of a tree's root system—both horizontally across the site and vertically within what is called the soil profile—an exploratory trench is carefully dug parallel to the curb. After removing the old asphalt, city workers discovered in the case of the two redwood trees an extensive and "spongy" mat of roots just below the

144

asphalt that did not extend very deep into the soil profile due to the naturally poorly drained soils in that part of Eugene.

Because the Hilyard Street project involved a complete reconstruction of the street, from the crushed rock base to the new layers of asphalt atop the crushed rock, the necessary excavation to a depth of 34 inches would have required the removal of the under-street portion of the redwoods' root mass, which could have killed the trees in the process—or at least rendered them potentially very unstable. But in an effort to protect the trees, public works engineers chose instead to reconstruct that portion of Hilyard Street with just a six-inch layer of reinforced concrete directly atop the root mass, creating a "root bridge" that protects the trees' roots and ensures their continued health.

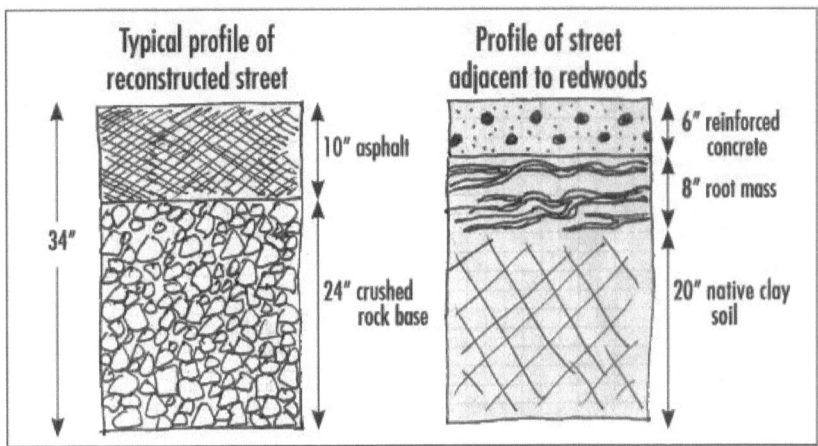

So next time you are in the 1600 block of Hilyard Street, take a closer look at the two coast redwoods on the east side of the street and the bright white concrete section in the street itself. And be thankful that we live in a community that cares enough about its trees to find innovative ways to protect and preserve them, even during major projects that in the past— and in most other communities—would have likely required their removal.

(Please turn the page to see a photograph of the Hilyard Street project.)

A City of Eugene crew examines the extent of the redwood roots by using a water jet to remove the soil and expose the roots.

(This article first appeared in the Summer 2008 edition of *ETF News*.)

THE REMOVAL OF A HEALTHY TREE
SHOULD ALWAYS BE A DIFFICULT DECISION

W HEN I MOVED INTO MY HOUSE on Potter Street in 1998, a friend suggested—when she first saw the house and the magnificent two-trunked coast redwood out front—that I had actually bought the *tree*, and the house just came with it! Indeed, the tree dominates my property and is loved by all who visit or pass by my house. Despite its size, though, the redwood is younger than I am, having been planted around 1960.

Soon after moving into the house, I had the redwood's two trunks cabled together, which is a relatively common and widely accepted arboricultural practice. I did this because of the inherently weak "crotch" of multi-trunked conifers—and my concern for both life and property, since the house stands northeast of the redwood, or downwind of it during winter storms. In the ten years that have elapsed since then, I have dutifully watered the tree twice monthly during our annual summer drought— because redwoods are native to the coastal Fog Belt and need summertime moisture in order to maintain their health—and I have watched the tree grow bigger and bigger.

Like the tree itself, the risk of living downwind of it has continued to grow, too, until I now feel that I can no longer accept that risk. Removing a perfectly healthy tree is not something that a tree lover like me ever really wants to do, and the expense of its removal is considerable. So coming to a decision about the tree has been a long and arduous process for me.

But I have finally decided to have the redwood removed in October 2008, and will see to it that every part of the tree is put to good use after it is felled. Dimensional lumber from the trunk will be sawn on-site after the felling, and the chipped rot-resistant branches will be made available to neighbors for mulching or to use for garden paths. Plus, several "rounds" of the two trunks will be made into tabletops. In short, I want the redwood to "live on" in as many forms as possible after it is gone.

In the ten years that I have lived in my house, I have planted more than two dozen trees in the front yard that are ready to help fill the void created by the departing redwood. In addition, I plan to plant a half-dozen more where the redwood now stands.

For ETF's fall 2008 newsletter, I shall write an article describing in more detail the removal process, but because none of us tree lovers likes a "surprise" (that is, the sudden disappearance of an old tree friend), I wanted to announce my plans—to readers, neighbors, and passersby—well in advance of the tree's removal.

(This article first appeared in the Summer 2008 edition of *ETF News*.)

A HOLE IN THE SKY—A HOLE IN MY HEART: REFLECTIONS ON THE REMOVAL OF A LARGE TREE

AN ARTICLE IN THE SUMMER 2008 ETF NEWSLETTER—The Removal of a Healthy Tree Should Always Be a Difficult Decision—announced the pending removal of a large, healthy, coast redwood tree (*Sequoia sempervirens*) from my front yard. The decision had been a difficult one, as the tree had become a veritable neighborhood monument and its branches provided a deeply shaded oasis for passersby.

But as the two-trunked redwood grew bigger, so did the risk of the inherently weak juncture of the two trunks failing during a storm, and one or both of its huge trunks crashing down on nearby dwellings. In the end, I decided it was my responsibility—knowing what I know about trees—to say farewell to this gentle giant.

Because of the redwood's exceptional beauty, I purposely designed my entryway to include a slight jog which forced visitors to turn and "behold" the tree from beneath, in all its magnificence. And I designed a bench that encouraged them to linger longer and enjoy the tranquility of the special space the tree created.

Over the years, many other people were drawn to the tree. For months, a letter carrier daily parked his vehicle and enjoyed his lunch in the tree's ample shade. More than one young mother nursed her infant while seated on the bench. And one day, I returned to my home to find a man—who apparently did not have a home of his own—sleeping beneath the tree; I didn't disturb him.

But it wasn't until the redwood's removal was imminent that I truly realized the magnitude of its gifts to so many people. I posted adjacent to the sidewalk a large, fluorescent-yellow sign that explained what was going to happen. And I delivered fliers to all the houses within about a one-block radius. In the weeks preceding the removal, scores of people stopped by to pay their respects.

Two days before the planned removal, as I headed out on an errand, I saw an older woman who passes my house daily on her walk around the neighborhood and I stopped to say hello to her. I asked her if she knew what was going to happen to the redwood. She did not, even though she had been walking within inches of the bright yellow sign for several weeks. I could tell that my revelation shocked her, but I left her alone with the tree and continued on my errand.

Early the next morning, when I went outside, I found an envelope taped to my mailbox beneath the tree. I sat down on the bench to read it:

> *Dear Whitey,*
>
> *Please accept my heartfelt condolences on the imminent demise of your beloved coast redwood tree. We all will miss it very much. I have always enjoyed looking at and smelling that beautiful and majestic tree...*
>
> *I am, a grateful neighbor R.*

Here was written proof of how trees can affect people. This woman's words helped me to forget temporarily the somewhat heartless assertion of another neighbor a few days earlier who said, "Whitey, you may be the only person who really cares about this tree . . . most people probably don't even notice it."

In anticipation of the tree's removal, I dismantled the fence beneath it to permit the workers easy access for removing the redwood's many branches as they were sawn off and lowered to the ground. And I padded and covered the bench and mailbox—both anchored in concrete and unmovable—to protect them from accidental damage. Three tubs of still-vibrant impatiens got moved elsewhere. Understory plants that could be salvaged were transplanted. For the first time in many years, the area beneath the redwood no longer looked very inviting.

On its last evening of life, I placed ten luminarias—paper sacks weighted with sand, with candles in them—in a circle around the base of the redwood, one luminaria for each of the ten years I'd lived with the tree. As the nearly full moon rose that evening over the ridge to the east, it illuminated the redwood's canopy from above, while the light from the ten luminarias rose from below to meet the moonlight. It was a fitting farewell to a beloved tree.

(This article first appeared in the Fall 2008 edition of *ETF News*.)

IT'S DOGWOOD TIME AGAIN

ACROSS THE UNITED STATES, spring-flowering trees are very popular, both in residential gardens as well as along streets. Most of these trees are relatively diminutive—e.g., Japanese flowering cherries, flowering plums, and Callery pears.

One of the most popular of these trees is the dogwood, of the genus *Cornus*. In our area, nearly all of the dogwoods we plant are the non-native eastern flowering dogwood (*Cornus florida*), even though the native Pacific dogwood (*Cornus nuttallii*) is perfectly lovely. And the vast majority of eastern flowering dogwoods planted here are the pink variety.

Eastern flowering dogwood in full bloom.

I had to be careful not to say the pink-*flowered* variety, because the showy "petals" of dogwoods are actually *bracts*. Bracts are modified leaves

151

that play the role of petals by attracting the plant's insect pollinators, but they are not structurally part of the flower, as petals are. (Another very familiar example of a plant with showy bracts is the poinsettia.)

The flowers of dogwoods are very small and are borne in the central button of the *inflorescence*—which is what we call the whole contraption that includes the bracts as well as all of the flowers. Each flower has four tiny petals, and the flowers typically open well after the bracts have developed.

The inflorescence of eastern flowering dogwood always has four bracts, and the tree has a spreading habit. Pacific dogwood, on the other hand, has an inflorescence containing typically five to seven bracts, and the tree has a more vertical habit—with two or more ascending main trunks—and a canopy that is more oval in form.

Several tiny flowers are already open in the center of this Pacific dogwood inflorescence.

Interestingly, most of the named "varieties" of trees that we grow are in fact cultivars (short for *culti*-vated *var*-ieties), but the pink dogwood is a *true* variety. That is, unlike cultivars which exist only in cultivation, the pink dogwood occurs naturally in the wild. And it also breeds true from seed; that is, if you plant the seed of a pink dogwood, the progeny are all virtually identical to the parent (not so with cultivars!).

Because it is a true variety, pink-flowered dogwood's botanical name is written *Cornus florida rubra*, all italicized. Cultivar names, on the other hand, are always written in plain text and, when part of a botanical name, are capitalized and enclosed by *single* quotation marks. So if the pink dogwood were actually a natural mutation that had occurred in a nursery—i.e., a cultivar—and was propagated by grafting, its botanical name would be *Cornus florida* 'Rubra'.

As beautiful as dogwoods can be in residential landscapes here in the Willamette Valley, they make poor street-side trees. The two species mentioned above are susceptible to anthracnose—a fungal disease that can defoliate the trees—and both are intolerant of the poorly drained soils we find in some areas of our community. The relatively small stature and spreading habit of the eastern flowering dogwood, in particular, make it difficult to provide the required clearance above sidewalks and streets for pedestrians and vehicles.

The eastern species also requires summer irrigation to thrive here, and tends to do best when protected from the strong afternoon sun, conditions that are seldom met in street-side planting strips.

(This article first appeared in the Spring 2012 newsletter of *Friends of Trees*.)

PLANTING TREES IN STRAIGHT LINES:
IS IT THE LAW?

FOLLOWING A RECENT TOUR of the new John E. Jaqua Academic Center on the University of Oregon campus, the young guide made some concluding remarks about the building's design, and thanked all of us visitors for coming. We were standing once again by the front doors, where the tour had begun, and I asked her, "But what about the new landscape outside? Aren't you going to tell us about that?" No, she said, she hadn't been told by her supervisors to say anything about it.

Drat! Once outside, I had wanted to ask her if she knew why most of the new trees were planted in straight lines of a single species, and all the trees within each line were evenly spaced. I know she wouldn't have had an answer, except perhaps, "Well, that's just how trees are supposed to be planted."

No, it is not. Although straight lines of evenly spaced trees of a single species may have their place—at the Palace of Versailles outside of Paris, for example—it is only one of many planting design options. So why do we see it virtually everywhere on commercial and institutional properties?

Look across the street from the Jaqua Center at the new Matthew Knight Arena. Although ample green space was provided around the building, all the trees are lined up once again. And, despite the large planting area, only two species are used: columnar European hornbeam and green ash. And why no trees native to the Willamette Valley? The arena's landscape doesn't say *anything* about Eugene, Oregon; it could just as well be in Denver or Boston.

Elsewhere around our community, it's the same story. Parking lots, schools, the Hult Center. Look at the drawings for Lane Community

College's new building across from the Eugene Public Library: more green blobs lined up like soldiers on parade.

Thankfully, the landscape architect for the new Wayne L. Morse United States Courthouse decided to mass trees in a somewhat more "natural" arrangement, at least on the west and north sides of the building, where scores of native incense-cedars and European beeches (and a few aspens) were planted to provide an aesthetic as well as acoustical buffer to the unattractive and noisy Ferry Street Bridge viaduct just to the west of the building. But elsewhere—on the building's east and south sides—it's single-species plantings, evenly spaced, and usually in straight lines.

So much in our cities is rigid and rectilinear: building façades, utility lines, curbs, sidewalks. Why can't the trees at least be planted in such a way that they soften that rectilinearity rather than add to it? It is not difficult to do, and it would make the lives of the designers and architects a bit more interesting. As a designer myself, I am aware that the design of more informal "naturalistic" plantings takes more time and thought than conventional cookie-cutter design. But I find the work very satisfying. Did I study landscape design to plant trees only in straight rows? Surely not.

One landscape architect tells me that he specifies plants to be in rows of the same species so that they are easier to count when verifying that the contractor doing the landscape installation planted the requisite number of each species. I thought he was joking! (He was not.) I'm hopeful that this article will spur other designers to present me and ETF with more defensible reasons for continuing this style of planting.

What are some alternatives to linear plantings? Even if the space allotted for trees is long and relatively narrow—which, curiously and sadly, is frequently the case—one can cluster trees of one species in part of the planting, choose a second species with different spacing elsewhere in the planting, and so on. God never decreed that all trees must be planted twenty or thirty feet apart. In fact, He sometimes plants them Himself *three* feet or *eighteen* feet and three and a half *inches* apart. We can do the same, and the result, like most of wild Nature, is likely to be very pleasing to the eye.

All of us appreciate some predictability in our lives. But we're also grateful for little surprises. So it is when planting trees. Go ahead and plant four or five trees in a line in a narrow bed. Then plant two more fairly close together and at a different angle, in a separate little bed—as if they "hopped out" of the main bed just to be different.

Better yet, encourage architects to design more ample space for trees around their buildings. One or several large beds are better—from the trees' point of view, for ample rooting space—than many small beds, or narrow beds, or, worst of all, trees imprisoned by steel grates.

Most important, however, is that we bring to the attention of others, as often as possible, the idea that there is nothing *wrong* with planting straight lines of evenly spaced trees of a single species, it's just that there are so many *other* options! Why not make designers' lives—and those of the admiring public—a little more interesting by exercising some of those options now and then?

(This article first appeared in the summer 2011 edition of *ETF News*.)

FALL IS POLLINATION TIME FOR ATLAS CEDARS

ALTHOUGH MOST TREE SPECIES in Eugene bloom in spring and early summer, one can count on finding at least one or two species blooming somewhere in the area during every season of the year. Many conifers, in particular, bloom during late fall and winter.

(Because conifers or needle-leafed trees are not true flowering plants, it is technically incorrect to refer to their reproductive structures—pollen or "male" cones and seed or "female" cones—as "flowers" or to say that they "bloom," but I'm going to do it anyway.)

In general, conifers have showier pollen cones than seed cones—at least at the time pollination is occurring and before the seed cones begin to develop. Atlas cedars (*Cedrus atlantica*) have exceptionally large and showy pollen cones, sometimes three inches in length and up to half an inch in diameter. The cones first become visible in late summer, and by October they ripen and disseminate their pollen.

The spent pollen cones are most noticeable after they have fallen, when they carpet the ground beneath the tree with what look like big, fuzzy, yellow caterpillars. But by then, their work is done and, if all goes well, the tree's then barely visible seed cones will have been fertilized and, the following growing season, will grow into the large, barrel-shaped, upright cones that we typically associate with all of the true cedars (Atlas, Himalayan or deodar, and cedar-of-Lebanon).

To my knowledge, the Atlas cedar is the only tree of African origin that we cultivate in the Eugene area. It occurs naturally in the Atlas Mountains (no surprise there!) of Morocco and Algeria where, like Colorado spruce, most trees have green needles, but variants with bluish foliage can also be found. And, again like Colorado spruce, we seldom see the green form in cultivation; instead, the blue form or cultivar (*Cedrus atlantica* 'Glauca') is grafted onto a green-needled seedling so the entire tree will have bluish foliage as it develops.

Immature pollen cones of Atlas cedar in September.

The vast majority of the cedars grown in the maritime Pacific Northwest are green-needled Himalayan cedars (*Cedrus deodara*) with much longer needles and an overall droopier appearance to the tree. But keep your eyes open for blue Atlas cedars, especially in mid-fall, when the pollination season for this species reaches its peak.

(This article first appeared in the Fall 2010 edition of *ETF News*.)

ETF CELEBRATES ITS
TENTH ANNIVERSARY

SHORTLY AFTER DAWN on June 1, 1997, the Sunday morning quiet of downtown Eugene and the neighborhood just west of it was broken by the sound of chain saws. Only a few hours later, 40 large trees—mostly sweetgums and bigleaf maples—lay wilting in the early summer sun, and the landscape of West Broadway between Charnelton and Lincoln streets was changed forever.

What had been two city-owned parking lots was to become the future Broadway Place development. And although the removal of the trees was legal and had been much discussed during the preceding months, many Eugeneans were still horrified to see the shady city block turned into what looked like a battlefield—the corpses, in this case, being those of the trees.

One of the people who never again wanted to see such carnage was Jon Kline, who resides just a few blocks west of the site. Jon had planted trees with Friends of Eugene's Urban Forest (a group that planted and advocated for trees during the late 1980s and early 1990s) and was profoundly aware of the benefits that large trees provide in urban areas.

Jon telephoned a half-dozen of us who had been active in earlier pro-tree efforts, and on Tuesday evening, July 15th, we met at Jon's house to discuss the formation of what would eventually become Eugene Tree Foundation. From the outset, we agreed that our group would strive to act always in a constructive and respectful manner when advocating for trees. The schism here in Eugene between the development community and environmentalists was already considerable; our hope was to bring diverse interest groups together, not further separate them.

Since its earliest days, ETF has had a three-pointed approach to helping ensure a more tree-friendly and tree-filled community. First and perhaps foremost is our very popular and successful tree planting program—including the Trees-for-Concrete projects where concrete in the public right-of-way is removed and trees are planted. These plantings are made possible by the City of Eugene's NeighborWoods program (started in 1992) which provides the trees; ETF members and others who help plant them; and the always supportive and helpful staff of the division of urban forestry within the city's Public Works Department.

East 11th Avenue at Pearl Street—the first Trees-for-Concrete project—on a sunny day in April 2007.

The second part of ETF's mission is its education program, from providing slide shows to interested community groups, to publishing a quarterly newsletter which is mailed out to more than 800 people and businesses.

The third part of our mission is advocating on behalf of trees. Some of the major downtown projects where we have had significant influence include the Eugene Public Library, the re-opening of Broadway between Oak and Charnelton, and most recently, the new plantings at the Citizens Building at 10th and Oak. ETF has become a respected voice in our community and we work comfortably and amicably with developers and environmentalists (not necessarily mutually exclusive groups), city staff, and local utilities to ensure that trees are always part of the discussion.

Meanwhile, Eugene's landscape continues to change, just as it always has. Old trees sometimes must be removed, and new trees are planted. Before 1850, the corner of Broadway and Charnelton was a treeless grassland as a result of frequent fires set by Willamette Valley native peoples to maintain the open, mostly treeless (!) landscape that they favored.

From the late 1870s until well into the 1900s, the four corners of the intersection were homes to some of Eugene's most prominent citizens, including the T. G. Hendricks family. A drawing of the Hendricks home from the early 1880s clearly shows vigorous young bigleaf maples growing in the park strip in front of the house. (*Author note: See the image on page three of this volume.*)

As Eugene's downtown changed in the mid- to late-1900s, the houses and the trees at Broadway and Charnelton were removed to make way for new businesses—and new trees. The two lots west of Charnelton eventually became parking lots for cars, under a canopy of maturing trees.

Then those trees were cut in 1997 to make way for the new apartments and yet more trees—including new bigleaf maples right at the intersection of Broadway and Charnelton—were planted. A 1997 inventory of trees growing in the public right-of-way in downtown Eugene showed many empty spaces just waiting for trees. Now, just ten years later, virtually every one of those spaces has been filled, thanks in large part to the efforts of Eugene Tree Foundation. Just imagine what we might accomplish in the *next* ten years.

Happy Anniversary, ETF!

(This article first appeared in the Spring 2007 edition of *ETF News.*)

SILK-TREE IS A NOSE TICKLER WITH ITS FLUFFY, PINK BLOSSOMS

MOST OF THE PLANT SPECIES AND CULTIVARS that grow in our area have a period of peak bloom that lasts about two weeks, whether they are Douglas-firs or daffodils. There are a few notable exceptions, however, to this general rule.

In the shrub realm, the one that comes to mind is glossy abelia (*Abelia x grandiflora*), a garden hybrid of two wild abelia species, hence the "x" in its scientific name. This broad-leafed evergreen shrub begins flowering as early as June and continues without break until November some years. Pretty amazing. Its pale pink flowers are small, but they make up for their size with sheer abundance and duration.

Glossy abelia is equally content in full sun and light shade and can easily grow to be ten feet tall and just as wide. Most gardeners, however, engage in the truly futile effort of keeping the shrub at four or five feet in height, or less. On some commercial sites, I even see these poor shrubs sheared into balls, completely destroying their natural fountain-like growth habit. Of course, this ensures "job security" for the people who do the shearing simply because the shrub refuses to grow as a ball.

The only locally grown tree with an extended period of bloom is the silk-tree (*Albizia julibrissin*). A native from Iran to eastern Asia, it is a fast-growing member of the pea family that lends a rather tropical appearance to some local landscapes. Its fern-like leaves are composed of hundreds of tiny green leaflets that fold up at night. This curious behavior may remind some people of the sensitive plant (*Mimosa pudica*), sometimes grown as a houseplant, with similar leaves that, even when touched lightly, close up in the same fashion.

The two plants are indeed closely related. In fact, in most places in the United States where they grow, silk-trees are usually called mimosas. But botanists and many horticulturists prefer the name silk-tree to distinguish the plant from the "true" mimosa or sensitive plant.

In addition to their attractive foliage, silk-trees produce a spectacular show of fluffy, pink, fragrant flowers that are real nose-ticklers, too, if you have the opportunity to stick your nose in one. The scent is especially strong on warm summer evenings. The trees begin flowering in July and continue well into September. Like other members of the pea family, the silk-tree's seeds are borne in flattened pods that are bright green during the growing season, then turn light brown in late fall. The pods are a distinctive feature of the tree well into winter.

Close-up of silk-tree blooms and foliage in mid-summer.

The leaves of most deciduous trees in our area lose their green-colored chlorophyll in fall and then reveal other colors like yellow and red that have been masked all summer by the more abundant green pigment. But the foliage of silk-trees remains green until it falls. In exceptional years, though, when we have an early and hard frost, the leaves may turn brown before falling.

To thrive, silk-trees need deep, well-drained soil and summer irrigation. If the location is to their liking, they can grow six feet or more per year during their youth and eventually reach a height of about forty feet. Compared to many other deciduous trees, however—such as oaks and maples—they are short-lived and seldom reach the age of fifty in good health.

These days, I generally discourage the planting of exotic (non-native) plants such as the silk-tree that both displace our native Willamette Valley plants—as well as the insects and animals that depend on them—and require a substantial amount of irrigation. Nonetheless, I still admire and appreciate very much the silk-trees that already grace area gardens. There are few scents as heavenly as that which emanates from a flowering silk-tree on a warm summer evening.

(This article first appeared in the 25 July 2001 edition of *The Springfield News*.)

IN PRAISE OF CONIFERS

BEFORE PREHISTORIC HUMANS ARRIVED here in the upper Willamette Valley, conifers already grew in abundance in this area. At that time, near the end of the most recent Ice Age, the landscape was much more open, with scattered groups of Engelman spruce and mountain hemlock separated by extensive grasslands where mammoths, giant ground sloths, and other now-extinct animals grazed and prospered.

But times change, and plant and animal communities change. With the dramatic warming of this area's climate that began about 10,000 years ago, the spruce and hemlock headed up into the Cascades, where the cooler climate better suits them, and Douglas-fir moved into the valley—presumably from the south—where it then persisted for millennia, despite the burning practices of area aborigines that kept much of this part of the valley in treeless prairie.

Douglas-fir now dominates local woodlands, and is joined sometimes by valley ponderosa pine, incense-cedar, and grand fir. But western hemlock and western redcedar—both of which are common farther north—are absent from our local forests.

The Euro-American settlers who began arriving in this area in the mid-1800s planted mostly native bigleaf maples along our streets because they were locally available, easy to transplant, grew fast, and developed broad-spreading, shade-providing canopies. But here and there, they also planted conifers. After all, conifers simply *belong* here, as they are perfectly adapted to our area's winter-wet and summer-dry climate. Part of what makes Eugene special is our urban forest that is composed largely of broad-leafed deciduous trees, but that is punctuated with the lofty spires of firs and incense-cedars, as well as giant sequoias and other conifers.

These days, people seldom plant conifers in their yards. And although City of Eugene regulations do permit the planting of conifers in the public right-of-way—with special permission from the City's Urban Forester—very few actually get planted. But that could be changing as people become more aware of the important environmental roles that conifers play. For example, unlike deciduous broad-leafed trees, evergreen conifers work year round—producing oxygen and storing up carbon through photosynthesis, and providing important stormwater benefits by intercepting precipitation in their dense canopies.

Particularly in Eugene's South Hills, homeowners and developers need to be encouraged to plant conifers. Otherwise, our distinctive conifer-cloaked ridgeline may end up looking very different by the next century. When an older fir is removed, we need to consider replacing it with another fir or other native conifer instead of a Japanese maple or eastern redbud. Future Eugeneans will thank us for thinking ahead and ensuring that conifers continue to be a substantial component of our urban forest.

(This article appeared in the Winter 2010 edition of *ETF News*; it was adapted from one that first appeared in the newsletter's Spring 2001 edition.)

PROLONGED OREGON FALL OFFERS A GREAT VARIETY OF VIBRANT COLORS

AND NOW, IT'S TIME FOR MY FAVORITE SEASON. Unlike many Willamette Valley residents who tolerate the rest of the year just to experience summer, I put up with summer just because I know that fall will be right on its heels.

I must admit, though, that I do appreciate the vegetable bounty that results from the warm and sunny days of summer, but I don't spend a lot of time outside except early in the morning and again in the evening. But once the sun starts to drop lower in the sky and the days begin to shorten, you'll find me outside more than in.

There are few places in the world where fall lasts as long as it does here, thanks to the influence of the Pacific Ocean. In the more continental climate of the Midwest, for example, fall seems to last just a few weeks, following closely the hot and humid days of summer and preceding by little the first snow of winter. But here, fall is usually evident already by mid-September and typically lingers until Thanksgiving or later, by which time the last deciduous trees are finally losing their leaves.

In addition to the pleasantly warm days and chilly nights, what I really like about fall is the quality of the light. It somehow seems to make the landscapes around us come into sharper focus than they were in summer. I've never been able to explain this, but that's just how it is and why I always look forward to this season. If you've ever lived in or visited more northerly latitudes during the summer, you know what I mean. The relatively low summer sun in Alaska and Canada and Scandinavia has the same stunning effect on the landscape.

Of course, another benefit of fall is the cleaner air that blows in from the Pacific, sweeping pollen, dust, and pollutants out of western Oregon's valleys and giving all the vegetation a good cleaning with the first light rains after the summer drought. In years when we go without any rain for two or three months or more, it is amazing the amount of dirt that accumulates on plants' leaves. Stand sometime under a big deciduous tree when it first begins to rain after a long drought and hold out a piece of white paper, and you'll see how filthy the drops are that fall from the leaves high in the tree's canopy.

For some people, fall can be a depressing time of year because, they say, many tender plants such as tomato and impatiens die with the first freeze, and trees become increasingly bare as their leaves drop. And then there's the rain. But as with everything else in life, it all depends on your perspective. I delight in watching the color changes that occur in deciduous leaves as their green chlorophyll breaks down and other pigments that have been masked all summer by the chlorophyll finally become visible.

Yellow xanthophyll pigments, orange carotenes, and red and purple anthocyanins have waited patiently all summer for this moment. And now that it's fall, these colors finally get their chance to appear and put on a big show just before the leaves fall. In addition to the spectacular oranges and reds of sugar maples and tupelos, be on the lookout for more subtle but equally beautiful colors such as the muted yellows of some trees and shrubs, and the beiges and browns of other plants. Remember, brown is a color, too.

For me, a special fall treat is the appearance of certain fungi. By that, I'm not thinking of the mushrooms that begin to sprout in the woods, although every one of them is fascinating to look at and some are quite tasty, too. What I'm referring to are some of the fungi that become prominent on leaves at this season.

One of my favorites is the aptly named tar spot fungus that appears on the leaves of many bigleaf maples. Although the fungus kills small, circular areas in the maple's leaves, it doesn't really "hurt" the tree, since the leaves by this time of year have finished most of their work and will soon drop anyway. Maple leaves with tar spot fungus are especially attractive, in my view, when backlit, which is of course the way one usually sees them when standing beneath a maple tree.

This fungus is so special that, as far as I know, it will grow on no plant other than the native bigleaf maple. If you've always thought that fungi other than edible mushrooms are just pests to get rid of, take a close look at one of your favorite bigleaf maples this October and I'm hopeful that you'll learn to look at fungi in a new way.

So join me in spending as much time outside as possible this fall. Too chilly for you? Put on a sweater. Too wet? Wear appropriate raingear or simply carry an umbrella. Confined to bed? Open the window several times a day and just enjoy the fresh air. There's simply no excuse for not being outdoors at this time of year, taking advantage of one of the most prolonged falls that our wonderful planet has to offer.

(This article first appeared in the 16 October 1999 edition of
The Springfield News.)

A DECIDUOUS "EVERGREEN"

WHEN REFERRING TO NEEDLE-LEAFED, cone-bearing trees, many people—if they are uncertain whether the trees are pines, spruces, hemlocks, or whatever—refer to the trees as *evergreens* (noun). The majority of cone-bearing trees or conifers are indeed evergreen (adjective), but some conifers are *deciduous*, losing all of their leaves every autumn just like broad-leafed trees such as maples and lindens.

The deciduous conifer we see planted most often in the Willamette Valley is the dawn redwood (*Metasequoia glyptostroboïdes*), a species that was once known only from fossils—including fossils found in central Oregon—and thought to have been long extinct until a small population of living dawn redwoods was discovered in a remote valley in southern China in the 1940s.

A second deciduous conifer is the larch or tamarack, one species of which is native to Oregon. The western larch (*Larix occidentalis*) is found mostly east of the Cascades, but grows perfectly well on the west side, if planted. Curiously, however, we see very few cultivated western larches or any other larch species, for that matter, here in the Willamette Valley.

The third and last major group of deciduous conifers is the bald-cypresses. One species, *Taxodium distichum*, is occasionally planted in our area. A swamp-land native from southern Delaware to the Gulf Coast, west to Texas, and then up the Mississippi Valley as far as southern Illinois, the bald-cypress actually grows just as well on upland and well-drained sites as it does on water-logged soils.

Like all deciduous conifers, the needles of bald-cypress are relatively thin in cross-section and bright green in color. The needles, after all, need to last only one growing season, so they never develop the toughness associated with the needles of evergreen conifers which must remain on the tree through at least one winter and sometimes several or more.

One very accessible place to see bald-cypresses in our area is near the Chambers Street overpass, on the slope just southeast of the traffic light where Chambers becomes River Road, and where the access road to Railroad Boulevard curves downslope from the light. This cluster of about a dozen trees has an interesting history. In the early 1990s, I received the trees as ten-inch-tall seedlings as a membership gift from the National Arbor Day Foundation. Although I had no room for them in my own garden, I didn't want to just throw them in the compost pile, so I planted them temporarily at my place and let them develop for a couple of years.

In the meantime, I noticed that the over-irrigated and then-treeless bank at the Chambers site was filled with water-loving horsetail and was very soggy year round. "Nothing" would grow there—other than the somewhat unwanted horsetails. So I asked permission from the City of Eugene to plant the bald-cypresses on the site, and the trees have thrived.

The delicate, deciduous foliage of bald-cypress.

Several years after I planted the trees, someone planted a dawn redwood out in the middle of the adjacent grassy area. So it's a good place to see both species of deciduous conifer right next to each other, and compare and contrast the two.

A unique attribute of bald-cypresses is their habit of forming "knees" when growing in or near water. These woody growths arise from the trees' roots and sometimes reach a foot or more above water level. Properly called *pneumatophores*, their function is unclear. When planted on upland sites, however, the trees seldom develop knees unless the soil is waterlogged. The best place to see bald-cypress knees in our area is along the south edge of the University of Oregon "Duck Pond" across Franklin

Boulevard from Lawrence Hall, where a half-dozen trees are planted pond-side.

*Bald-cypress knees (foreground) and the distinctive buttressed base of
the parent tree—when growing in or near water—in the background.
(Photo taken along the south side of the Duck Pond north of Franklin Boulevard.)*

The largest and oldest bald-cypress I am aware of in our area can be seen along the west edge of Tugman Park, on the far side of the little stream that runs by just beyond the hexagonal picnic shelters. Although the site is at least seasonally wet, the tree has never developed any knees. And, like the Chambers site, there are two dawn redwoods of about the same height just behind the bald-cypress, but they are very poorly developed due apparently to the confined space of the site. Also at Tugman, in a small bed on the south side of the park, is a lovely *young* bald-cypress that was planted about fifteen years ago.

There are at least two sites in Springfield, as well, where one can easily see this tree. One is at the intersection of Pioneer Parkway and Centennial Boulevard. A total of eight bald-cypresses can be seen at three of the four corners of the intersection with the most stunning individual at the northwest corner. Then, way out in an industrial area in east Springfield—in a seasonally wet swale just northwest of the intersection of Olympic Street and 40th Street—is a sweet little grove of a half-dozen young bald-cypresses. How did they get there? I have no idea.

Like other deciduous conifers, bald-cypresses occasionally suffer "untimely deaths" when property owners notice that their cone-bearing "evergreens" suddenly lose all their needles in late fall, and they ask to have the trees cut down! Let's hope that doesn't happen to any of the trees mentioned above. In the wild, bald-cypresses are known to live sometimes for well over a thousand years, so the relatively young bald-cypresses of our area have very long lives ahead of them, if we can just keep the chainsaws away.

(This article first appeared in the Fall 2011 newsletter of *Friends of Trees*.)

THE HARLEQUIN GLORYBOWER

MOST OF THE TREES AND SHRUBS that we grow in our area, both native and non-native, bloom for about two weeks of the year sometime between March and June. They attract our attention most when they are covered with flowers—presuming their flowers are indeed showy—then retreat into the background. So many different species bloom in spring that it can sometimes be a bit overwhelming. So much to see . . . so little time.

But things settle down dramatically as summer progresses, and few woody plants bloom here in late summer and early fall. So trees and shrubs that *do* bloom now tend to get plenty of attention, simply because there is so little competition.

Many of us are familiar with one of these late-bloomers, the silk-tree or mimosa (*Albizia julibrissin*). But there is at least one other woody plant that clamors for our attention in August and September, if you happen upon it. It's a small tree that more than compensates for its diminutive stature with a common name nearly as long as its botanical name. It's the harlequin glorybower (*Clerodendrum trichotomum*). The adjective harlequin usually refers to something that is variegated in pattern. In this plant's case, the fruits which follow the tubular white flowers are stunning: iridescent, turquoise berries that are surrounded by magenta, star-shaped calyces (the parts of flowers that support the petals and the rest). Wow!

The glorybower part of the name refers to the glorious bowers of flowers that these trees become in August. Although individual flowers are less than an inch across, they are borne in very showy clusters. But these little trees often get your attention long before you see them, thanks to the intense fragrance of their flowers.

On top of all these attributes is my favorite one of all. It's the leaves. They are purplish when they emerge and are covered with a wonderfully soft fuzz. But wait, there's more. When you gently rub the new leaves—especially the smallest ones at the tips of the branches in summer—then place your fingers to your nose, you smell peanut butter. I kid you not. (I've never read about this in any horticultural text; when it comes to fragrance, most horticulturists, it seems, are so focused on a plant's flowers that they forget to smell its leaves.)

By now, some of you may have thrown this paper onto the living room floor and are in your cars headed for the nearest nursery. And I'm not surprised. What does surprise me is that we see so few of these trees in our area. For a long time, they were simply unavailable in local nurseries. That has changed somewhat in the past few years, but you still have to look pretty hard to find one of them.

The harlequin glorybower is a lovely small tree that seldom exceeds 10–12 feet in height.

Although established trees are rare in the southern Willamette Valley, they are more common farther north, especially in the older neighborhoods of Portland. I don't know why this is, except that Oregon's nursery industry is centered farther north so people there may have access to a greater variety of plants than we do.

At any rate, if you are captivated by this little tree and can indeed find one to purchase, it needs to be planted in a sunny to lightly shaded location with well-drained soil. Once established, the tree is relatively drought tolerant, which is always a plus. One of the tree's shortcomings, in the minds of some gardeners, is its tendency to sucker, not from the base of the trunk but from the roots some distance from the trunk. But I can certainly live with that.

The tree grows fairly fast when young and soon acquires a rounded crown. It can eventually reach a height of about fifteen feet and a width of about the same. And because of its suckering habit, a single tree can eventually develop into a small grove. (In Eugene, there is one of these little groves along the West Bank bicycle path, just where it turns off Copping Street to head to the Owosso bike bridge.)

In areas with colder winters than we usually have, the harlequin glorybower is sometimes grown as an "herbaceous perennial." That is, it is cut down at the end of each season—or freezes back on its own—then it re-sprouts the following spring and, since it blooms on what is called "new wood" produced during the current year, it will flower in late summer, just like the tree does. Even in our area, you can grow the plant like this if you'd rather not have a tree.

The list of this tree's attributes is long: flowers that are intensely fragrant and appear in late summer when few other woody plants bloom; fruits that are a dazzling combination of turquoise and magenta; leaves that smell like peanut butter; a diminutive stature so the tree can fit on almost any lot. My gosh, is there anything this plant does *not* do? Yes, there is one thing: Its leaves do not change color in fall before dropping. Oh, well—can't have everything.

(This article first appeared in the 21 August 2002 edition of
The Springfield News.)

BUILDING IN NATURE'S ENVELOPE

THE WOODED LOT FOR SALE in Eugene's south hills was a picture of paradise. Tall Douglas-firs shaded a rich undercanopy of vine maple, western hazel, and sword fern. Wildflowers carpeted the ground in spring and a great variety of birds, insects, and other animals took advantage of the food and cover that the site naturally provided.

No one had planted these trees or the other plants or put out feeders to attract the birds. No one ever watered the shrubs or fertilized the wildflowers. Because it was a naturally healthy biological community, no serious pests ever developed and no weeds grew on the site. And it didn't cost a cent to maintain. Paradise, indeed!

The people who eventually bought the lot considered it paradise, too. They pictured their future home nestled in the trees and enveloped by the site's stunning natural beauty. What they did not realize was that, to make that dream come true, they needed to carefully protect the site's existing landscape at every step of the construction process.

Instead, they focused on getting a bank loan, designing the house, and choosing kitchen cabinetry. Meanwhile, the bulldozer arrived and began to rearrange the hilly site's soil to accommodate the house foundation, carving holes out of the hillside in one area and then piling that soil around the trees lower on the site, effectively smothering their roots. And while the bulldozer was at the site, the contractor decided to do the owners a favor and remove all the "brush" from among the trees, thus removing the site's well-established and perfectly healthy undercanopy.

By the time I arrived on the scene to discuss "landscaping" with the owners, there was not much I could do. Despite the owners' request that the site be damaged "as little as possible," they had not taken adequate steps to protect the site's valuable natural features, so those features were lost.

Building in nature's envelope—where the site's pre-existing natural features actually envelop the finished building—permits machinery and other activities only within the so-called footprint of the future building and in a narrow "transition zone" from two feet to five feet in width that extends beyond the building footprint. This means installing a sturdy exclosure or fence to protect the site and imposing hefty fines for any violations.

But building within the envelope means, too, that the design of the house and any outbuildings must affect as little of the site as possible—build small and tall instead of sprawling the house across the site. Ask yourself if you really need four bedrooms and three baths for a family of four. And instead of having an attached garage and the driveway that such a garage requires to connect it with the street, why not place the garage adjacent to the street and connect it to the house with a path? Or create a shared garage space with several other neighbors?

This house on Nectar Way in south Eugene was carefully built to preserve the site's natural features.

Rather than build your house in the center of the lot, thus reducing the natural area to fringes around the lot's perimeter, how about moving the house to one side or corner of the lot and leaving a bigger chunk of natural area? And instead of building on a slab or conventional foundation, consider building at least part of the house on pillars or posts. This reduces the building's effect on the site's hydrology (how water flows underground through the soil) and also helps protect the roots of existing trees.

Keep in mind that the reason you bought the lot in the first place was its natural beauty and make every effort at every step of the way to protect and preserve what nature provides for you for free.

Developing a site in this fashion can add to the cost of development. But that cost is more than offset by having an intact, fully functional landscape already in place after construction is completed.

The environmental and economic benefits of this approach are considerable, yet most Eugene homeowners and builders continue to build as we always have before. We scrape the site clean, rearrange the soil, and build the house as if it's the only thing that matters, then pay to haul in new soil and plants and hope for the best. What usually results is a dysfunctional landscape that requires constant pampering and the application of water, fertilizer and pesticides to ensure its survival.

Even on *unwooded* sites, this approach should still be applied. Where former agricultural land is being developed on the valley floor, for example, it is just as important to designate protected areas to ensure that the soil of future landscaped areas is not abused during site preparation and construction activities.

If you plan to build a new home and wish to preserve the site's natural character, be very clear with your contractor. If he suggests that your concern is unwarranted or that driving machinery across the soil and among the trees "won't really hurt anything," find yourself another contractor. Because by choosing to build in nature's envelope, not only will the resulting landscape look and function better, but it will make you and your contractor look better, too, because you cared enough about the site's natural amenities to protect them throughout the development process.

(This article first appeared in the Fall 2005 edition of *ETF News*.)

A GIFT OF GINKGOS

EVERY LIVING TREE HAS A UNIQUE STORY—when and where it germinated (or was grafted), when or if it was transplanted, the events that have transpired in its branches and adjacent to it, and so on. Likewise, each human being has a unique story unlike that of any other person in the history of the planet. But it's the intersection of trees' stories with those of humans that can be especially intriguing.

Such is the case of the two ginkgo trees at the northwest corner of East 13th Avenue and Hilyard Street. Planted nearly half a century ago and spared at the last moment during the redevelopment of the site in the late 1980s, their story is unknown to the thousands of people who daily pass by the trees.

Like the ginkgos themselves, the people who planted them were immigrants to the United States from China. Both Rose Tsou and her husband, Leslie Tsou—whom she met at the University of Washington in Seattle—grew up in China under comfortable circumstances, and attended prestigious Chinese universities where they received their bachelor degrees. Toward the end of World War II, Leslie was invited to the U.S. to serve as an interpreter for American troops who were going to be sent to China to help oust the Japanese. But before he could perform that service, the war ended—after the dropping of the atomic bombs—and he ended up staying in the U.S. to attend graduate school.

Meanwhile, back in China, Rose finished her undergraduate degree in journalism and had the opportunity to come to the U.S. to complete a second BA in English literature and an MA in library science. She arrived in Seattle in early 1947, where she eventually met and married Leslie.

Despite their degrees, the Tsous found it difficult to obtain jobs in their fields—due in part to their limited English, but also because they were Chinese. At the invitation of a Chinese-born University of Oregon professor, whom Rose had known in China, the young couple visited Eugene in 1955 and soon thereafter moved here and found themselves proprietors of a small, but until then poorly run Chinese restaurant in the 1200 block of Alder Street.

Both Rose and Leslie worked energetically to turn the restaurant into a profitable business, and in 1960, with the help of the Calkins family, regular customers at the restaurant, they were able to purchase at a very favorable price one of the Calkins family's houses at 13th and Hilyard, where the Tsous then lived until they had enough money to demolish the house—which was in poor condition—and build their own restaurant, since they had been renting the space on Alder.

The Tsous hired Chinese-born Corvallis architect, Edith Yang, to design the building in classic Chinese style, and Dick Chambers—another loyal restaurant customer—to build it. They decided to extend the building's Chinese motif to the landscape around it, and heavily planted the entry to the restaurant with plants native to China.

Although many kinds of ornamental trees that grow well in our area are native to China, Leslie decided to plant ginkgo trees in front of the restaurant along Hilyard Street. It was not easy at that time to find ginkgos in local nurseries, but he eventually acquired four young trees and planted two of them—the ones we still see today, both females—in front of the restaurant. (The other two, both males, were planted at the Tsou family's residence at the corner of East 29th Place and Elinor Street, where they continue to thrive.)

Whitey Lueck and Rose Tsou visiting the two ginkgo trees at 13th and Hilyard in fall 2009 and discovering—upon seeing the fruits on the trees—that the trees are in fact females, not males, as previously thought.

The Tsous owned Leslie's Mandarin Restaurant until 1980, when they sold it. Then, in the late 1980s, the entire city block where the restaurant was located was to be redeveloped. All of the buildings were slated for demolition, and all of the trees—including the two ginkgos planted by the Tsous—were to be cut.

At that time, Eugene had a Tree Commission—an advisory group that worked with city staff to promote trees. One of its members, former Eugene mayor Ruth Bascom, advocated for the preservation of the two ginkgos. Ruth's special fondness for ginkgos had begun in the early 1960s when her physician-husband, Dr. John Bascom, had his practice in an office building at 10th and Mill. A single ginkgo grew in the parking lot north of the building (and still does) and, in fall, delighted everyone when its foliage turned brilliant gold just before dropping. The Bascoms had also become good friends with the Tsous; in fact, over the years, three of the four Bascom daughters worked for the Tsous as waitresses.

Rose Tsou, whose family planted the trees some 50 years ago, seen here with her beloved ginkgos.

Thanks to Ruth's advocacy on behalf of the two ginkgos, the developers of the new Physicians and Surgeons Center agreed to spare the trees. Unfortunately, however, the trees were not protected at all during construction activities, but they managed to survive despite the damage done both to their trunks and to their roots. (On the west side of the trunk of the southernmost ginkgo, one can see the remains of a large wound that, even twenty years later, has still not closed over completely.)

Eugeneans who have lived here for an extended period are linked in countless ways to one another and to the wondrous landscape that surrounds us. And the longer we live here, the more intricate and complex those connections become. For most people, the intersection at 13th and Hilyard is like any other: You arrive by car or by bike or by foot, you wait for the green light, and you move on. While you wait, you might notice the greenery at the northwest corner, but it's just a backdrop to the hustle-bustle going on around it.

From now on, however, when at least some of us pass through that traffic intersection, we will be reminded of the intersection of the lives of Ruth and Rose and the two ginkgos.

(This article first appeared in the Fall 2009 edition of *ETF News*.)

SKINNER BUTTE WALKING TOUR

I INITIALLY DEVELOPED THIS TOUR in the spring of 2005, the first year I taught my Trees Across Oregon course at the University of Oregon. Our first off-campus field trip in that course is to Skinner Butte Park, where we begin our walk down by the river, ascend the butte through the forested north-facing slope, then descend the much more open south-facing slope and return to our starting point at Lamb Cottage via the residential East Skinner Butte Neighborhood.

The visit to Skinner Butte Park introduces my students (and perhaps the reader of this book, as well) to: 1) One of Eugene's premier parks, located at the geographic center of our community; 2) a variety of both native and non-native trees; 3) an overview of Eugene's history; 4) Eugene's three major soil types (each of which supports tree growth differently); and 5) a park and neighborhood of rich and varied landscapes.

The tour and map here are of course just a snapshot in time, as the landscape changes continuously. The most recent revision was made in May of 2017. For the location of the numbered stops below, please refer to the map that follows the text.

THE TOUR

(Enjoy your visit—virtual or otherwise!)

1. **Riparian woodland**: Soil Class A (River Soil: deep, fertile, and well-drained). Dominant trees: bigleaf maple (*Acer macrophyllum*), Oregon ash (*Fraxinus latifolia*), willows (*Salix* spp.), cottonwood (*Populus trichocarpa*), and the occasional Douglas-fir (*Pseudotsuga menziesii*) higher on the bank. The riverside woodland ecology is changing dramatically as cottonwoods, alders, and willows

184

disappear because the upriver dams have now all but eliminated the natural disturbances (floods) which used to open up new gravel bars and sand bars which these trees need for germination.

2. **Toe-slope of Skinner Butte**: Soil Class C (Wetland Soil: poorly drained clay-like soil derived from Mt. Mazama volcanic ash). Dominant tree: Oregon white oak (*Quercus garryana*). Non-native trees that are doing well here include dawn-redwood (*Metasequoia glyptostroboïdes*) and red maple (*Acer rubrum*), both of which are native to naturally wet sites. Note the native "wet prairie" restoration site east of Lamb Cottage—an excellent alternative here to manicured lawn.

3. **The new forest**: Until the 1850s, the butte was mostly grassland— with many species of native wildflowers, but only a few scattered oaks and apparently no conifers at all. After the once-frequent Indian-set fires ended, Douglas-fir seeded in quickly onto the butte's north slope from trees growing along the river, so the trees in this forest date mostly from the 1850s. Some grand fir (*Abies grandis*) seeded in, too, but all of the large ones have died from uncertain causes during the past decade or two. Bigleaf maple is common in the middle canopy. Shrubs include vine maple, Indian-plum, red elderberry, and snowberry. Soil Class B (Hill Soil: moderately well-drained, but relatively shallow).

4. **Herbaceous layer**: From March through June, the forest floor here is carpeted with wildflowers including candyflower, fringecup, false Solomon's seal, fairy bells, trillium, and many others. Most of these had disappeared during the decades-long English ivy era (mid-1900s through early 2000s), but have rebounded impressively following removal of the ivy.

5. **Non-native plants**: Besides English ivy, one can see near this hairpin in the path Portugal laurel (*Prunus lusitanica*), sweet cherry (*Prunus avium*), Norway maple (*Acer platanoides*), and English holly (*Ilex aquifolium*), all of which are displacing native Willamette Valley forest plants as these non-natives become established. Note, too, a half-dozen small grand firs downhill from the path here; these trees are between 50 and 75 years old, but grow extremely slowly in the shaded undercanopy here . . . just waiting their turns to "take off" once one or two of the nearby tall Douglas-firs dies or blows over.

6. **Old oaks**: These two Oregon white oaks—both of which were severely disfigured in the ice-storm of December 2016—are likely over 200 years old, despite their relatively small stature, due to the extreme conditions (shallow soil and extended summer drought) in which they grow. Note the old fire scar at the base of the south tree. Indian fires? A settler's campfire? The scar has still not completely closed over (or "healed") in the last 100-plus years.

7. **Young oaks**: The trees in the open area atop the butte were planted in April 1999 to establish a new generation of oaks. The same day, at the meadow's east end, two bigleaf maples were also planted to develop broad canopies out in the open and to eventually "frame" the view from the parking area to the new oaks—but only one survives, and it's struggling due to the thin soil and increasingly severe summertime drought of this site, as Eugene's climate changes.

8. **The 1934 plantings**: Hundreds of different trees—mostly conifers not native to this area—were planted on the butte's south slope in an effort to "beautify" what was at that time still a mostly treeless area. Notable survivors visible here include giant sequoia (*Sequoiadendron giganteum*) from California's Sierra; until recently, Port-Orford-cedar (*Chamaecyparis lawsoniana*), all of which have now died due to a root fungus; Atlas cedar (*Cedrus atlantica*) from northwestern Africa; and two extremely rare maritime pines (*Pinus pinaster*), one of which was declining rapidly in 2017 from bark beetles, and both with naturally leaning trunks.

9. **Incense-cedar woodland**: This very dense stand seeded in from the dozen or so large incense-cedars (*Calocedrus decurrens*) that were planted around the Shelton-McMurphey-Johnson house in the late 1880s or earliest 1890s.

10. **Shelton-McMurphey-Johnson house trees**: Besides the notable incense-cedars, observe the large Oregon-myrtle (*Umbellularia californica*) southwest of the house, and the extremely rare western white pine (*Pinus monticola*)—a two-trunked individual "embraced" by a bigleaf maple southeast of the house.

11. **Campbell House**: Notable Himalayan cedar (*Cedrus deodara*) and Oregon white oak.

12. **High Alley plantings**: Giant sequoia with a bite out of it to allow utility wires to pass by it, and rare (in town) western hemlock (*Tsuga heterophylla*).

13. **The future**: What might the Skinner Butte (and environs) landscape look like in 50 or 100 years . . . ? The only certainty is that it will look different than it does today.

(Please turn the page for the tour map.)

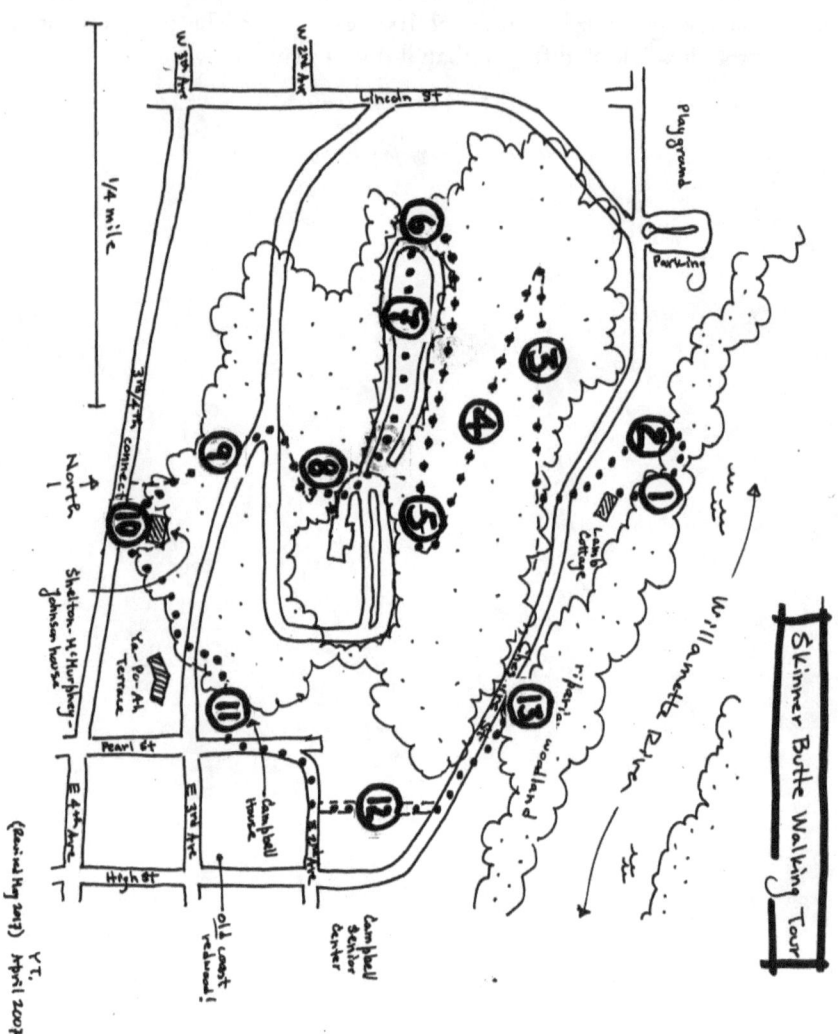

CARING FOR TREES AND SERVING THE PLANET: AN EARTH DAY MESSAGE

I CELEBRATED EARTH DAY a bit early this year when an elderly neighbor decided to uproot a three-foot-tall Oregon white oak that had been planted a couple of years ago in the park strip in front of her house. It turns out that she was losing sleep over the thought of all the fallen leaves that she would someday, in her advancing years, have to rake up.

I have to admit that I rolled my eyes when I heard this and I was tempted to go right over and "have words" with the dear octogenarian. Instead, I rolled up my sleeves, grabbed a shovel, and replanted the young tree in a formerly treeless spot on the *other* side of the street. Happy Earth Day!

As a long-time and completely out-of-the-closet dendrophile (or "tree-lover") I have heard over the years just about every excuse imaginable for not liking trees in general, or a certain tree or species of tree in particular. I honestly try to "embrace," as we say these days, such diversity of perspective. But frankly, it is just plain difficult for me to understand.

Caring for the land—and for the trees that grow on it—is an ethic that I learned as a child. I can't help it: My father was one of the renowned conservationist Aldo Leopold's students at the University of Wisconsin during the early 1940s. People like us believe that the natural world that surrounds us is our collective living room, and it is our shared responsibility to care for it in the best way we know possible. And that includes planting and caring for trees, both on our own properties as well as on public property. It's the least we can do, no?

Almost every other holiday we celebrate in our American culture involves giving something to someone: candy on Valentine's Day; flowers on Mothers' Day; neckties on Fathers' Day; and of course all kinds of presents at Christmas. And sure, many of these holidays also involve appreciation and gratefulness. But Earth Day is about giving something *back* to the planet from which we humans *take* so much. As ETF's education chair illustrates in his column on page three, there is truly no end to what trees do for us—both in the utilitarian as well as the aesthetic and spiritual sense.

Most everyone recognizes this. But some people prefer their trees at a distance, preferably on the opposite side of the street rather than in their own yards—as long as the leaves don't blow back across the street to their yard. One can only presume that these same people appreciate children, but only if someone else changes their diapers and rears them. (Children, like trees, can sometimes be so "messy," you know.)

European horsechestnuts along the west side of Jefferson Street.

Passersby sometimes shake their heads in disbelief when they see me outside raking leaves or planting trees or pruning. A typical remark is, "Boy, you sure have *your* work cut out for you!" They can't believe that I am actually enjoying what I'm doing. But like everything else in life, it's all about attitude. The work I do with trees is healthy—I'm outside and exercising my body and often my mind as well—and extremely satisfying. It is work, yes. But it is joy-filled work, and that is something that too few people these days get to do.

The next time you're outside "caring for creation"—even if it's your own garden-esque creation—make sure to smile so that passersby know that you're doing it because you want to, not because you have to.

I'm glad that I didn't "have words" with my neighbor. By focusing my energy instead on replanting the oak tree—especially in a spot where she can still see it—I am hopeful that my actions will serve to get the Earth Day message across in a more subtle and enduring way.

(This article first appeared in the Spring 2009 edition of *ETF News.*)

TREES AND NEIGHBORHOOD REDESIGN

S EVERAL YEARS AGO, I WAS ASKED to give a talk about trees and neighborhoods, and how I—drawing on my background in horticulture, ecology, and landscape design—might redesign an existing neighborhood, or design a new one, to better provide for the needs of trees as well as people.

One of my chief concerns about the current state of residential landscaping is that it is far too people-oriented and largely ignores the needs of the rest of our community: native plants and animals that once called this part of the upper Willamette Valley "home."

To most people, the term "habitat loss" brings to mind tropical jungles being bulldozed and turned into cattle farms to grow cheap beef for North Americans' burgers. But we ignore the habitat loss that has occurred in our own yards due to the construction of our homes and the creation of landscapes—dominated by lawns, non-native trees (and other plants), and bark mulch—that attract very few of the native critters that once lived here, and displace all the rest.

My second major concern regards tree species selection and tree placement. Most trees are selected based solely on their aesthetic attributes. Pretty trees are great, but how about selecting trees based on their environmental and ecological roles *in addition to* their appearance?

Where tree placement is concerned, trees are very often planted where they could eventually shade a neighbor's vegetable garden, the much-loved sunny patio, or the solar panels on the roof, again because we are so focused on beauty that we largely ignore the functions and effects of trees and how those change over time.

So what could we do? First of all, in typical valley-floor neighborhoods, we could designate front yards as a giant "forest reserve" and replant them using appropriate native trees—for example, Douglas-fir and bigleaf maple on well-drained river loam soils; and Oregon ash, aspen, and ponderosa pine on poorly drained soils farther away from the river, nearer the hills. The result would be forested corridors stretching for blocks and blocks and from front door to front door. Although mostly on private land, the forest reserves would be planted and cared for according to a city-created master plan and trees would be harvested on a sustainable basis to provide lumber and other wood products. Yes, that's right: we would all have a productive "working forest" right in our front yards.

In some areas, oak/pine savanna with an understory of native grassland (grasses and wildflowers) would supplant the denser, closed-canopy forests with their undercanopies of native shrubs and herbaceous plants. But whatever the details, the so-called "streetscape" would be devoted to habitat restoration while simultaneously shading the street—to keep the neighborhood cooler in summer—and the front sides of all the houses.

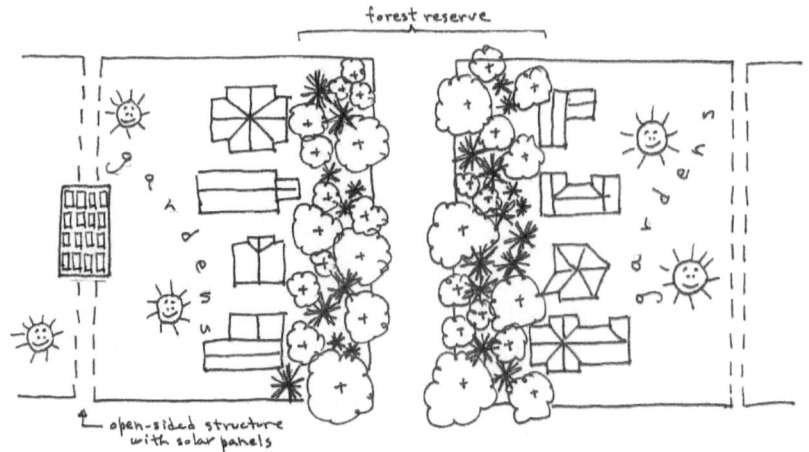

Plan view of one block of a redesigned neighborhood.

Having paid our collective debt to nature by converting our formerly dysfunctional front yards into attractive and biologically productive wildlife habitat, we could then turn our attention to our backyards, which would be devoted largely to human needs. First and foremost is food production, which requires lots of sunshine and no competition from large trees—either above ground (due to the trees' shade) or below ground (tree roots take water and nutrients that your food plants need).

Another use for sunny backyards and rooftops is electricity production with solar panels. Mounted atop roofs, they produce a secondary benefit by shading the house in summer and helping to keep it cooler. Neighbors might also consider installing solar panels atop an open-sided structure where adjacent backyards converge to create a meeting-place beneath, perhaps with picnic tables and a storage area for shared tools.

The advantages of this proposed scheme are many:

- Habitat restoration
- Neighborhood cooling (in summer)
- Social benefits of neighbors working together toward a common goal
- In-town lumber production
- Water conservation (little or no irrigation necessary in the forest reserves)
- Solar energy production (largely unimpeded by trees)
- Educational benefits of neighbors learning to understand, appreciate, and care for wildlife habitat adjacent to their own homes

I realize, of course, that the communitarian ideals expressed in this proposal may not sit well with people raised in a country that values individual rights so highly. Yet most of us already have a publicly owned "park strip" in front of our residences that we get to care for along guidelines determined by our community. Narrowing those guidelines—to include only those native plants suited for the forest reserve—and expanding that same management philosophy up to our front doors is not that big of a jump, is it? And most of us already appreciate the importance of habitat restoration, even if we don't yet know how to do it on our own properties.

Elevation view of street-side forest reserve.

The early pioneers who came to the salubrious Willamette Valley thought they had found "Eden." Imagine a visitor arriving in Eugene fifty or one hundred years from now and finding neighborhoods laced with beautiful, native woodlands and, in backyards, productive gardens providing most of the fresh fruits and vegetables consumed by the happy households who live here. An earthly paradise, indeed!

(This article first appeared in the Summer 2009 edition of *ETF News*.)

A LETTER FROM THE TREE FAIRIES

I N MID-1997, WHEN I LEARNED that our local transit district was planning to plant mostly northern red oaks at its new downtown Eugene Station, I contacted the organization in an effort to dissuade them from planting that species because of its prodigious crop of acorns some years, which would be both a mess and a liability at a busy urban bus station. But my words fell on deaf ears—as they sometimes do.

So I decided that I needed to use a different approach—one that maybe didn't directly involve me or other humans—to get the attention of our decision-makers. And I called on my long-time buddies, the Tree Fairies, to see what *they* could do to relay my concern about the proposed oaks.

And here is the letter the fairies (ahem!) wrote. I then asked a sweet female friend of mine with a well-developed sense of humor to put on a nice dress and deliver to each of the four people below a little basket of acorns along with a copy of the letter.

The letter paper had the following heading:

Tree Fairies
Helping Humans Better Understand *The Real World*

And the paper's footing said:

No address
No telephone
No need . . . because we're *everywhere*!

Here's the letter:

22 September 1997

Phyllis Loobey, General Manager (Lane Transit District)
Harriet Cherry, Project Manager (WGBS Architecture)
Vicki Elmer (City Manager)
Don Bishoff (The Register-Guard)

Happy Autumn, Dear Friends:

Permit us to introduce ourselves. We're Tree Fairies. Don't be embarrassed if you've never heard of us before. Like most humans these days, you were probably simply unaware of our presence—indeed, our omnipresence! But we're busy wherever you humans are building something, doing what we can to ensure that whatever you're building incorporates trees in a thoughtful manner. Occasionally, we need to ask a human to act on our behalf, simply to remind you that we're out here. To that end, we have asked a human who "speaks fairy" to deliver to you this little basket-o'-nuts.

As you know, Lane Transit District is in the process of building a new bus terminal in downtown Eugene. Although most of the site will regrettably be covered with concrete, there will be a few trees planted to help make the area a somewhat more pleasant place to be. One of the tree species selected for this site is the northern red oak. This oak is an incredibly beautiful tree (although, quite frankly, we Tree Fairies can't think of *any* tree that is *not* beautiful) that is native to the forests east of the Great Plains. So you see, it really doesn't belong here in the upper Willamette Valley. But many people like it so much that they plant it here anyway.

Young trees spend most of their time developing a good root system and a nice canopy. But by adolescence, a red oak's thoughts—like those of so many other adolescents—turn to, well, reproduction! The adolescent tree's first attempts at reproducing are somewhat limited—a few acorns here, a few acorns there. Eventually, however, the tree gets the hang of it and goes into full production.

If you're an oak, acorns are wonderful things. They're the only means you have of passing on your genes to the next generation. But if you're a human being transferring from one bus to another at a busy downtown plaza shaded by red oaks, it can be something quite different. Humans using the plaza may benefit all summer long from the oaks' shade without giving the trees a second thought. But come September, they will be reminded just where that shade came from when it begins to rain acorns. Some humans will then refer to the otherwise innocent reproductive efforts of the oaks as a "maintenance problem" or, worse, a "liability."

There will be suggestions that the "awful" trees be cut down. Other humans will chain themselves to the trees to keep them from being cut, and recommend instead that the plaza just be closed every year for the month of September. Questions will be asked of those people originally involved with the project (if they're still in town): Didn't they know any better? It'll be quite a mess. And we're not talking about the acorns!

To get a feel, so to speak, of what the future holds if red oaks are indeed planted, as planned, at the LTD site, we suggest that you:

- Find a smooth surface such as a linoleum hallway floor or a concrete sidewalk, and scatter the acorns in this basket on the ground in front of you. Then try to walk across the acorns to get to the other side of them. Careful, now . . . since fairies don't believe in lawsuits, you can't blame *us* if you fall!

- Have a friend or co-worker drop a dozen or so of these acorns onto your (unprotected) head from a balcony or upper-story window that is at least 20 feet above you. Ouch!

After performing these two simple activities, try to imagine how Eugeneans will feel twenty years from now as they skitter on and get bonked by acorns from the red oaks that were planted back in the 1990s by people who didn't listen to the Tree Fairies. Oh, my. If you're still not convinced, take a little field trip to the northwest corner of West Eighth Avenue and Madison Street (the source of the acorns in your baskets) where it's raining acorns right now. And don't forget to wear your knee pads, elbow pads, and protective helmets this time!

So please, for the sake of both the trees and the people, kindly reconsider the selection of red oaks for the new LTD plaza. We think you'll be glad you did.

All our best,

The Tree Fairies

Postscript

Don Bishoff—who wrote a weekly column for *The Register-Guard*—decided to write a column about the Tree Fairies' suggestion. (I don't recall if Don knew yet that I was in cahoots with the Tree Fairies—but maybe he suspected it, as I was pretty well known around town for my pro-tree antics.) That column caused a bit of public embarrassment for those involved with the project, which in the end proved to be very effective at getting my point across.

And a few weeks later, LTD submitted a revised landscape plan to the City of Eugene which specified a half-dozen Japanese zelkovas, a half-dozen green ashes, and . . . a single northern red oak for the site. The Tree Fairies had prevailed once again.

Long live the Tree Fairies!

ABOUT THE AUTHOR

Whitey Lueck was born and grew up in Pennsylvania—first in Jersey Shore, a small town in the mountains of the north-central part of the state, and later in Lancaster in the southeastern part of the state. He left the U.S. in 1974 after graduating with a degree in horticulture from Pennsylvania State University. In northern Sweden, he milked cows on a small farm and picked berries in the surrounding forests. He then interned as a horticulturist and landscape designer for municipal parks departments in Nantes, France, and in Bern, Switzerland, before returning to the U.S. in 1977 to attend graduate school at Oregon State University in Corvallis, where he eventually completed a double masters in forest ecology and German. He has lived in western Oregon ever since, except for a two-year hiatus at the University of Wisconsin in Madison in the early 1980s.

The author of countless articles and a popular speaker about trees and what he calls "the world around us," Whitey began formally writing essays in 2004. His first collection of essays—published in 2015 and called *Staying Put in Lane County*—recounted his activities and musings during the 2014 calendar year when he purposely never left his home county. In 2016, he published *Words from the Woods: 2004–2008*, followed in 2017 by *Words from the Woods: 2009–2011*, and also in 2017 by *Sixty-four Trips Around the Sun*.

Whitey teaches part-time at the University of Oregon in the Department of Landscape Architecture, and lives not far from campus on a very nature-friendly property that is open to the public and showcases a household that produces all of its own fruits and vegetables (as well as eggs and honey), makes its own electricity (from rooftop solar panels), and has no driveway (because Whitey has never owned a car).